Academia's Billion-Dollar Roulette

This book explores how in a rapidly shifting world, higher education has found itself at the crux of socioeconomic, demographic, and technological transformations. This book dives deep into this evolving landscape, navigating the vast complexities of global higher education and its cultural implications.

From demographic challenges and economic pressures to the game-changing implications of artificial intelligence, this book paints a holistic picture, highlighting the intersections and potential futures of academia. Equipped with meticulous research, global case studies, and enlightening expert opinions, this book offers a rich tapestry of insights that cater to a diverse array of readers. As universities grapple with uncertainties, this book emerges as a compass, offering actionable insights, strategies, and foresight into the transformative potential of various factors. It's not just a diagnosis of the current state but also a prescription for the road ahead.

This book distinguishes itself as a unique and essential discourse in the realm of educational literature, presenting a rich, multidimensional analysis of the crossroads at which higher education currently stands. This book is not just an academic treatise; it is a clarion call to action, urging universities, policymakers, educators, and students to engage deeply with the transformative challenges and opportunities presented by the digital age.

This book is tailored for a broad spectrum of readers including higher education policymakers, university administrators, and educators who will find it particularly invaluable. Yet, its accessible language and engaging narratives also appeal to students, and anyone curious about the trajectory of higher education in our rapidly changing world.

Ken-Tye Yong is a professor at the University of Sydney, specializing in Chemical and Biological Engineering. His innovative research spans nanotechnology, biophotonics, and nanomedicine, leading to over 350 publications and numerous awards. Alongside his academic achievements, Ken-Tye's entrepreneurial efforts and deep interest in astronomy further define his versatile career.

Morning Liu is a postdoctoral researcher at the University of Sydney, who blends industry experience with academic research. Specializing in embedded software for wireless networks, she transitioned to academia focusing on neural activity modeling. Her current research involves biophysical models and machine learning in protein dynamics.

Academia's Billion-Dollar Roulette

Ken-Tye Yong and Morning Liu

Routledge
Taylor & Francis Group
LONDON AND NEW YORK

First published 2025
by Routledge
4 Park Square, Milton Park, Abingdon, Oxon OX14 4RN

and by Routledge
605 Third Avenue, New York, NY 10158

Routledge is an imprint of the Taylor & Francis Group, an informa business

© 2025 Ken-Tye Yong and Morning Liu

The right of Ken-Tye Yong and Morning Liu to be identified as authors of this work has been asserted in accordance with sections 77 and 78 of the Copyright, Designs and Patents Act 1988.

All rights reserved. No part of this book may be reprinted or reproduced or utilised in any form or by any electronic, mechanical, or other means, now known or hereafter invented, including photocopying and recording, or in any information storage or retrieval system, without permission in writing from the publishers.

Trademark notice: Product or corporate names may be trademarks or registered trademarks, and are used only for identification and explanation without intent to infringe.

British Library Cataloguing-in-Publication Data
A catalogue record for this book is available from the British Library

ISBN: 9781032759869 (hbk)
ISBN: 9781032759906 (pbk)
ISBN: 9781003476504 (ebk)

DOI: 10.4324/9781003476504

Typeset in Times New Roman
by codeMantra

Contents

	Acknowledgments	vii
	Introduction	1
1	The Looming Storm	2
2	Universities in the Crosshairs of Global Trade and Economics	9
3	The Great Divide	17
4	The High Price of Higher Learning	28
5	The Age of Upheaval	36
6	When AI Stakes Its Claim in Higher Education	48
7	Balancing the Scale: AI-Led Education's Promise and Perils	56
8	Charting a New Course	63
9	University in 3-D: Academia, Society, and Personal Growth	73
10	Bracing for the Twenties: Challenges of the Decade	82
11	Intriguing Prelude	96
	Index	*105*

Acknowledgments

I express my profound gratitude to a constellation of distinguished individuals whose insights and discussions have been invaluable in shaping the themes of this book. I extend my heartfelt thanks to Willy Zwaenepoel for his foresight on the future of universities and the leadership required in these transformative times. Special appreciation goes to Paras Prasad, Mark T. Swihart, Masahiko Inami, Benjamin Eggleton, Hugh Durrant-Whyte, and Sandra Margon whose expertise on the intersection of artificial intelligence, machine learning, and higher education has been instrumental. Their perspectives on navigating an aging society and fostering innovative research are deeply appreciated.

I am also immensely grateful to Zhong Lin Wang and Ben Zhong Tang for their visionary thinking about how future technologies will enhance student and university growth. Their perspectives on harnessing potential in a competitive environment have been enlightening. I would also like to express my gratitude to Ben Thornber, whose insightful views on the equal importance of basic and applied science for advancing technologies across all areas have significantly contributed to promoting innovation and a transformative learning experience for students. Furthermore, I extend my heartfelt thanks to Bunty Avieson for her relentless support, encouragement, and strong friendship. Her guidance in writing and publishing this book has been invaluable, and I am profoundly thankful for her assistance.

I am also grateful to Robert Langer, Eric Mazur, and Paul Weiss for the opportunity to visit in their laboratories during my tenure as a visiting scholar. The experience in their labs has enabled me to approach problems from various angles and lenses, fostering a mindset that is creative, bold, and responsible. Most importantly, it has instilled in me a commitment to devise sensible, adaptable, and sustainable solutions to our daily challenges. This approach ensures that future generations can build upon our innovations with creativity and excellence, without the need to reinvent the wheel.

Throughout my academic career, my colleagues and friends – Lee Pooi See, Yoon Soon Fatt, Teng Joon Lim, Hesham El-Gamal, Ibrahim Abdulhalim, Ling Ye, Shawn Chen, Kuan Wang, Wing Cheung Law, Chih Kuang Chen, Aaron Ho, Gaixia Xu, Peter Han Joo Chong, Indrajit Roy, Shubha

Shukla, Wun Jern Ng, Din Ping Tsai, Anirban Maitra, Anusha Withana, Le Ba Tan, Deanna D'Alessandro, Joseph Haus, Edward Furlani, Rose Amal, Folarin Erogbogbo, Donghyun Kim, and many others – have established a robust platform for debate and discussion. Their contributions have significantly enhanced my understanding of university governance and policy.

A special note of thanks to my past students, whose journeys and achievements fill me with pride and whose insights into university life have been a source of continuous learning and inspiration. Your successes and meaningful careers are a testament to the enduring value of higher education.

My colleagues at USYD deserve a special mention for their collaborative spirit and commitment to shaping a resilient and forward-thinking academic environment. Our collective wisdom and efforts are a driving force in building universities that not only serve our country but also inspire global collaboration.

In conclusion, this book is a tribute to the collective wisdom and dedication of all those who strive for excellence in higher education. As we say, with good intentions and diligent efforts, we forge ahead toward a brighter future for universities worldwide.

Introduction

In *Academia's Billion-Dollar Roulette*, we embark on an exploratory journey into the transformative world of higher education, a domain standing at a crossroads amid the relentless waves of technological and societal change. This book delves into the critical role of universities as they navigate the uncharted territories of artificial intelligence (AI) integration, demographic shifts, and the digital divide. At its heart, this narrative scrutinizes the delicate balance between preserving the human essence of teaching and harnessing the formidable capabilities of artificial intelligence. It poses probing questions. Can universities adapt their venerable traditions to the demands of a rapidly evolving global landscape? Will they embrace the digital dawn or succumb to the perils of obsolescence?

Through vivid analyses and compelling insights, *Academia's Billion-Dollar Roulette* offers a panoramic view of the challenges and opportunities that lie ahead. It explores the intricate dance of adapting to AI-driven education, the urgent need to bridge the digital divide, and the perennial quest for balancing technological advancements with the irreplaceable value of human interaction. This book is an invitation to ponder the future of education, a future where universities must not only impart knowledge but also ignite creativity, foster critical thinking, and prepare students for an unpredictable world.

Readers will find themselves immersed in a thought-provoking narrative that not only highlights the current state of higher education but also envisions its future. It's a compelling read for educators, students, policymakers, and anyone interested in the trajectory of higher education in an era marked by technological upheaval and societal change. Join us in unraveling the complexities of this billion-dollar roulette, where the stakes are high, and the outcomes will shape generations to come.

1 The Looming Storm

Spinning the Wheel: The High-Stakes Gamble of Modern Academia in an Age of Uncertainty

In the grand casinos of the mind, where intellect and innovation jostle for supremacy, there exists a table that draws a crowd unlike any other. Here, the stakes are higher; the risks are more profound; and the players are an eclectic blend of dreamers, disruptors, traditionalists, and trailblazers. Welcome to academia's billion-dollar roulette – a metaphorical game of chance, strategy, and sheer audacity, where the wheel spins on the axis of change, and the bets are placed on the future.

The roulette wheel symbolizes the unpredictability of life, a concept that resonates deeply within academia. Universities are currently facing a series of significant challenges due to rapid changes in technology, unstable economic conditions, and shifts in societal norms. Their focus is primarily on four key areas: advancing research, improving education, fostering collaboration, and developing a forward-thinking vision. Success in these areas isn't measured in financial terms but rather through the contributions they make to knowledge, their impact on society, and their influence on the education and development of future generations. These institutions play an essential role in adapting to and shaping the ever-changing landscape, ensuring they remain relevant and effective in a world that constantly presents new challenges and opportunities.

But as in any game of chance, the wheel is impartial, and the outcomes can be both exhilarating and brutal. Universities, the architects of knowledge and the incubators of innovation, now stand at the crossroads, facing a dilemma that is as existential as it is compelling. Will they embrace the winds of change, adapt to the new paradigms, and thrive in the chaos of the twenty-first century? In response, universities, seizing these winds of change, are poised to evolve. By integrating cutting-edge technologies and interdisciplinary approaches, they flourish in the dynamic landscape of the twenty-first century, transforming into vanguards of progress and adaptability. Or will they falter, weighed down by tradition and complacency, and find themselves fading into the footnotes of history? Conversely, if mired in tradition and complacency, these bastions of learning risk obsolescence. Slowly receding into the shadows of history, they may be remembered more for what they were than for what they could have become.

As the world spins ever faster, propelled by the relentless march of technology and globalization, universities find themselves at this pivotal juncture. This moment teems with both peril and promise. The choices made now will not only shape their destinies but also reverberate through the annals of human progress. To navigate this uncertainty, universities must be nimble, ready to shed the past and emerge as beacons of innovation and adaptability. The future beckons, offering a chance to redefine their roles, not as mere repositories of wisdom but as active shapers of a world bristling with unknown possibilities.

The gamble is real, and the stakes are astronomical. The wheel is in motion; the bets are placed; and the world watches with anticipation, hope, and a hint of trepidation. In this intellectual contest, every spin could herald a breakthrough or a breakdown. It's a game where foresight, agility, and courage are the currency, and the dividends are measured in the enrichment of human potential.

The role of the university is being redefined, reshaped, and relentlessly questioned. The answers lie not in the wisdom of the past but in the audacity to imagine a new future. Successful universities are distinguishing themselves by embracing interdisciplinary learning, investing in technology-driven education, and fostering strong industry partnerships. In contrast, institutions falling behind often cling to outdated curricula, resist technological integration, and lack meaningful connections with the evolving job market. As you turn the pages, prepare to delve into an exploration of the strategies, challenges, triumphs, and tribulations of the institutions that dare to play academia's billion-dollar roulette. The game is on, and the wheel waits for no one. Welcome to the thrilling, turbulent, and transformative world of higher education in the age of uncertainty, where the divide between success and obsolescence becomes ever more apparent.

Cracks in the Ivory Tower: The Looming Crisis of Higher Education in a World Unraveled

Universities, the stalwart bastions of society's intellectual pursuit, stand on the brink of an existential crisis. An amalgam of pressing issues, as diverse as the disciplines they house, threatens to undermine their foundations. The storm is gaining strength, with decreasing birth rates, escalating economic pressures, and a desperate scramble to stay relevant in an era of unprecedented technological advancement. Despite the allure of online learning, universities offer irreplaceable experiences: the vibrant campus life that fosters critical thinking and social development, the opportunity for hands-on research and mentorship under esteemed experts, and the invaluable network of peers and professionals that extends far beyond virtual classrooms. These unique aspects of the university experience provide a compelling argument for their continued relevance, even as the digital age offers alternative paths to knowledge.

The proud tradition of universities dates back to the Middle Ages in Europe, where institutions like the University of Bologna and the University of Paris emerged to educate clergymen and bureaucrats.[1] As centuries passed, they transformed into sprawling centers of research and innovation, contributing significantly to societal progress. These institutions were autonomous, self-governing, and largely independent of church and state – a characteristic noted by historian Charles Homer Haskins in his groundbreaking work, "The Rise of Universities."[2]

But the beacon of stability has been flickering. Education news provider *Higher Ed Dive* – a specialized digital media outlet that delivers news and analysis on the latest trends, policies, and challenges in the higher education sector – reports more than fifty university closures or mergers in the United States alone between 2016 and 2021.[3] European institutions fare no better, according to the Higher Education Policy Institute. Southeast Asia also grapples with the crisis – in Indonesia, *The Jakarta Post* forecasts the potential closure of 529 private universities, thanks to dwindling enrollments and fiscal woes.[4] Thailand faces comparable challenges, while the Philippines and Malaysia also experience significant pressures that could impact the stability of their institutions.

Through this global catastrophe, the recurring villains – demographic shifts, economic tribulations, and ruthless competition – pose an existential threat to universities. The crisis, transgressing geographical and cultural lines, puts the very survival of these institutions at stake. As the situation deteriorates, it becomes evident that a radical overhaul of higher education's approach, financing, and structure is overdue.

Demographic challenges are at the heart of the unfolding crisis. Declining birth rates have begun to dry up the pool of prospective university students. This shift isn't a sudden occurrence; it's a culmination of social, economic, and political trends evolving over decades. Interestingly, while the pool of potential students shrinks, graduation rates have seen a nuanced trend. In many institutions, there's been a gradual increase in graduation rates, attributed to improved educational methods and stronger support systems. However, this increase is often offset by the overall decline in student enrollment numbers, leading to a net decrease in the total number of graduates. The result: a drastic decline in the number of high school graduates and a future marked by sparse college campuses.

With the onset of the COVID-19 pandemic, universities have been forced to adapt to online learning platforms and technological integration at an accelerated pace. The sudden shift exposed glaring gaps in technological preparedness, accessibility, and quality assurance. Universities had to contend with not only implementing new systems but also ensuring that students and faculty were equipped to engage in this transformed learning landscape. This development has led to a reconsideration of the role of technology in education and its potential to democratize access. However, concerns remain about the quality of online learning, the persistence of the digital divide, and the potential loss of the social aspects that physical campuses provide.[5]

A cocktail of influences is at work here. The push for financial stability and career establishment has resulted in delayed marriages and parenthood. Women, now more than ever, pursue higher education and career opportunities, often pushing childbearing to the back burner. Economic uncertainties, such as the financial crisis of 2008 and the ongoing COVID-19 pandemic, have discouraged couples from expanding their families.

Fiscal pressures tied to raising a child, urbanization, and evolving societal norms are changing family structures. The demographic transition triggered by these factors impacts various sectors, including higher education. The shrinking student base forces universities to scrutinize their roles, structures, and survival strategies.[6,7]

Economic turmoil exacerbates the higher education crisis. The above-mentioned combination of the 2008 financial crisis and the COVID-19 pandemic has wreaked havoc on public funding, squeezing university budgets. To make matters worse, the United States has seen a significant rise in tuition costs, over 14 percent in the last decade, as per the College Board.[8] Amid these financial challenges, the landscape of higher education delivery is also undergoing a dramatic shift. In 2020, 44 percent of students were enrolled entirely online, a steep rise from just 15 percent in 2019. Furthermore, the prevalence of blended-learning models is also on the rise, with 75 percent of students in 2020 taking some online courses, up from 36 percent the previous year.[9] These statistics underscore a rapidly evolving educational environment, where universities are increasingly offering stay-at-home degree programs to meet changing demands. The escalating costs have led to a burning question: how can universities strike a balance between quality, accessibility, affordability, and financial sustainability?

In countries like the United States, the escalating cost of higher education has resulted in a growing student debt crisis. According to Federal Reserve data, the US student loan debt reached nearly $1.6 trillion in 2021, affecting more than 44 million borrowers.[10] This financial burden has long-term implications for economic mobility and stability, particularly for marginalized and low-income populations. The crisis has ignited debates about the role of government in subsidizing education, the social contract between educational institutions and students, and the very value proposition of a university degree. It poses a fundamental question: is the financial burden of higher education justifiable in the face of uncertain economic returns?

In this changing landscape, the importance of a college degree to employers is also evolving. An increasing number of companies are now valuing "relevant experience" over traditional university qualifications, recognizing the diverse skills and perspectives brought by nontraditional candidates. This shift reflects a broader reevaluation of the role and value of higher education in preparing individuals for the workforce, challenging the long-held assumption that a university degree is the sole pathway to career success.

Political winds, too, exert a profound influence on the higher education landscape. Governments can manipulate funding, immigration regulations, and a university's overall orientation. As Derek Bok, former Harvard president, opines in his book *Universities in the Marketplace*, political pressures can push universities toward a market-driven model, often compromising their fundamental roles.[11]

This means that universities, under political influence, may start prioritizing financial gains and market trends over their core mission of education and research. As they align more with market demands, they risk deviating from their traditional roles as centers of learning and intellectual development, potentially sidelining academic rigor and critical thinking in favor of more profitable but less academically focused endeavors.

Economic crashes such as the 2008 financial crisis have triggered severe budget cuts, forcing universities to scout for alternative funding sources and passing costs onto students. Political ideologies and leadership changes also dramatically shift education policies. Migration policies, too, significantly affect universities, particularly in countries like the United States, UK, Australia, and Canada that host large international student populations.

Moreover, the rapid evolution of technology, giving birth to online learning platforms and alternative education providers, has challenged universities to stay relevant. As companies worldwide struggle to find adequately skilled employees, the divide between higher education and the labor market widens. Universities, traditionally focused on undergraduate and postgraduate education, must accommodate the concept of lifelong learning, essential in today's volatile job market.

However, the response of universities to this imperative has been mixed. While some institutions have pioneered innovative programs, forging partnerships with industries and embracing flexible learning models, others have struggled to adapt. The challenge lies not just in expanding their curriculum but also in aligning their educational models with the rapidly changing skillsets demanded by employers, thereby bridging the gap between academic training and practical workplace skills.

The modern challenges facing society demand interdisciplinary approaches and collaboration among various fields of study. Universities are increasingly recognizing the need to break down traditional silos and foster an environment where disciplines interact and converge. This shift toward a more interconnected academic structure reflects the complexities of issues like climate change, global health, and technology ethics. Universities must evolve to accommodate this trend, rethinking curricula, research paradigms, and institutional culture. Moreover, collaboration with industry, government, and nonacademic entities is becoming vital in translating academic research into tangible societal benefits. This shift represents both an opportunity and a challenge, requiring careful navigation to preserve academic integrity and independence.

Universities also grapple with the question of relevance in light of recent scientific advancements in artificial intelligence and data analytics, which are reshaping traditional teaching and learning methods. This invites the question: what will the role of professors be in the future of higher education? In the future, professors may transition from traditional lecturers to facilitators of learning, guiding students through complex problem-solving and critical-thinking exercises enhanced by AI tools. They could also become curators of personalized learning experiences, leveraging data analytics to tailor education to individual student needs and interests. Furthermore, professors might play a crucial role in bridging the gap between theoretical knowledge and practical application, integrating AI and data analytics into their teaching, to prepare students for a rapidly evolving job market.

As we stand on the precipice of these monumental shifts, we must ask ourselves, can universities, stalwarts of intellectual growth and pillars of society, adapt their structures and functions to accommodate these new realities? This is the question that will be explored throughout this book.

This exploration will reveal universities that are innovating aggressively, reimagining their curriculum and pedagogy to align with the digital age and globalized world. We will delve into case studies of institutions that are breaking traditional molds, forging new partnerships, and embedding lifelong learning and adaptability into their core missions. Through these examples, we will uncover not just the challenges but also the promising practices that signal a resilient and dynamic future for higher education.

This examination is necessary, for universities are not just institutions. They are a testament to our collective commitment to knowledge, growth, and societal progress.

References

1 H. de Ridder-Symoens, *A History of the University in Europe. Volume 1, Universities in the Middle Ages* (Cambridge: Cambridge University Press, 1991).
2 C. H. Haskins, *The Rise of Universities* (New York: Taylor and Francis, 2017).
3 "A Look at Trends in College Consolidation Since 2016," *Higher Education Dive*, accessed June 9, 2023, https://www.highereddive.com/news/how-many-colleges-and-universities-have-closed-since-2016/539379/.
4 "Number of Private Universities in Indonesia from 2013 to 2022," *Statista*, accessed June 9, 2023, https://www.statista.com/statistics/704753/number-of-private-universities-in-indonesia/.
5 "Understanding the Digital Equity Gap and Bridging the Digital Divide in Higher Ed," *EdTech*, accessed December 16, 2023, https://edtechmagazine.com/higher/article/2022/03/understanding-digital-equity-gap-and-bridging-digital-divide-higher-ed-perfcon.

6 N. D. Grawe, *Demographics and the Demand for Higher Education* (Baltimore: Johns Hopkins University Press, 2018).
7 "5 Changing Demographics in Higher Education," *NDM News*, accessed December 16, 2023, https://online.ndm.edu/news/education/changing-demographics-in-higher-education/.
8 J. Ma and M. Pender, *Trends in College Pricing and Student Aid 2021* (New York: College Board, 2021).
9 "Distance Learning," *National Centre for Education Statistics*, accessed December 16, 2023, https://nces.ed.gov/fastfacts/display.asp?id=80.
10 "Federal Student Loan Portfolio," accessed August 14, 2023, https://studentaid.gov/data-center/student/portfolio.
11 D. Bok, *Universities in the Marketplace: The Commercialization of Higher Education*, Vol. 49 (Princeton: Princeton University Press, 2003).

2 Universities in the Crosshairs of Global Trade and Economics

Global Economics: The Seismic Shift in University Funding

When the dust settled after the 2008 financial crisis, universities worldwide were left grappling with the harsh realities of their dwindling funds. Governments, reeling from the economic fallout, were forced to tighten their belts, and higher education bore the brunt of these austerity measures. According to a report by the Center on Budget and Policy Priorities,[1] by 2018, a decade after the crisis, the situation had not fully recovered. States were allocating $9 billion less to public higher education in 2018 than in 2008, reflecting the long-term financial strain and the ongoing consequences of the crisis on the higher-education sector.

Universities, desperate for a financial lifeline, found themselves considering alternative funding models.

Upping Tuition Fees

An obvious choice for many, increasing tuition fees could offset the loss in public funding. According to the College Board, there was a notable 37 percent increase in the average tuition at public four-year colleges in the United States from 2008 to 2018,[1] a surge that far exceeds the cumulative inflation rate of approximately 17.20 percent for the same period.[2] However, this tactic widened the educational chasm between the rich and the poor, causing a socioeconomic skew in the student body.

Private Funding

Relying on the goodwill of philanthropists, corporate sponsors, and private donors offered a potential financial respite. But these funds came with strings attached – concerns over the erosion of academic independence surfaced as research and academic directions appeared to be swayed by the preferences of the deep-pocketed donors.

Courting International Students

With their ability to pay higher tuition fees, international students became a lucrative target for universities. This ability often stems from the policies of universities and governments, where international students are charged premium rates compared to domestic students, reflecting nonsubsidized tuition costs. Additionally, many international students come from backgrounds where families have saved extensively or have access to funding specifically for overseas education, viewing it as a significant investment in future opportunities. Yet, this strategy was fraught with risk. Political tensions and fluctuating international student preferences left universities in a precarious position, underscoring the volatile nature of relying heavily on this demographic.

In Europe, universities encountered comparable financial difficulties. Italian universities faced a 20 percent drop in public funding from 2008 to 2015, as reported by the European University Association. Across the channel, the UK's Higher Education Funding Council reported a funding decrease of 25 percent during 2010 and 2015.[3]

Southeast Asia and Africa presented a different landscape due to their varying economic maturity. In Southeast Asian countries, private higher education institutions have proliferated to accommodate the increasing demand for advanced academic opportunities. Malaysia, for instance, has seen a significant surge in the number of private universities in the past two decades. Africa, constrained by limited resources, has wrestled with funding for higher education. South Africa and Kenya, however, have witnessed growth in private universities, while other countries have sought partnerships with international institutions to secure funding.

University funding is no longer a straightforward matter of public coffers. These institutions have to employ ingenuity and resourcefulness in their financial strategies, leading to a shift in research focus, student demographics, and access. These shifts have serious implications for social mobility, academic independence, and the future of higher education.

As the ripple effects of the 2008 financial crisis spread globally, countries like Japan, South Korea, Singapore, Indonesia, India, and China each charted unique courses, often shaped by their particular socioeconomic and political circumstances.

In Japan, the delicate balance of public and private funding for universities was disrupted, with an increase in private funding driven by higher tuition fees and greater private sector involvement. South Korea took the path of investing heavily in research and development, bolstering higher education funding. Singapore, small in size but with grand ambitions of becoming a global education hub, has maintained consistent funding for its universities, with the government's spending on education comprising $14.6 billion SGD (10.9 billion USD), representing 14 percent of the total government expenditure.[4]

Indonesia, saddled with a burgeoning youth population and a demand for higher education, struggled with the efficiency of its education budget. Meanwhile, India saw a surge in private sector involvement in higher education in the aftermath of the financial crisis. China, fueled by its economic growth, was able to significantly invest in higher education, helping Chinese universities ascend the global rankings.

The aftershocks of the financial crisis echoed the urgent need for universities to diversify their funding sources. The crisis also spotlighted how sociopolitical factors shape national responses and their effects on higher education. Despite a shared global economic blow, national contexts played a decisive role in the trajectory that universities took in response, leading to diverse consequences for access to and quality of higher education.

Impact of Trade Wars: The Sino-American Squabble Shakes Universities

China's star has been on the rise, with its economy hitting a full stride, particularly after joining the World Trade Organization in 2001. This monumental event heralded a new era in international higher education, one where China would come to play an increasingly significant role. Economic liberalization and a spot on the global trade stage filled China's coffers, and it wasn't long before its middle class began to balloon.

To give you a sense of the scale, the National Bureau of Statistics of China reported that the per capita disposable income catapulted from a meager 4,091 yuan (576 USD) in 2001 to an impressive 25,763 yuan (3,631 USD) in 2020. That's a sixfold increase.[5] McKinsey & Company projected that China's middle class would swell to encompass 520 million people by 2025.[6] With bulging wallets and a cultural premium placed on education, Chinese families began viewing overseas education as an attainable dream.

The Hurun Research Institute found that more than 60 percent of China's affluent folks had their sights set on foreign shores for their children's education. Mirroring this trend, the number of Chinese students flocking to US universities swelled. The Institute of International Education's Open Doors Report revealed a stark increase from about 60,000 Chinese students in the United States in the academic year 2000–01 to over 370,000 in the academic year 2019–20.[7] The figures were telling, clearly demonstrating the ripple effects of China's economic prosperity on the composition of international student bodies.

The story got better – the financial contribution of international students to the US economy was a cool $40 billion in the academic year 2022–23, with 27 percent coming from Chinese students.[8,9] Their areas of interest often mirrored global economic trends and China's quest for tech supremacy, with fields like business administration, engineering, and math and computer science being top choices.

But as the saying goes, "the best-laid plans of mice and men often go awry." The precarious trade relations between the United States and China, exacerbated by the Trump administration's hardline immigration policies, cast a long, uncertain shadow over the future of Chinese students in the United States. As per the National Bureau of Economic Research, the previously upward graph of Chinese student enrollment in the US took an 8 percent hit in 2018.[7] This marked the first downturn in over a decade.

This unsettling trend led Chinese students to scan the globe for friendlier academic harbors. Canada, for example, saw a surge of 22 percent in Chinese student enrollments in 2019, according to the Canadian Bureau for International Education.[10] Australia also saw a bump, with the Department of Education, Skills and Employment reporting a 10 percent increase in Chinese student enrollments in the same year.[11] In response to this shift, many US universities ramped up their recruitment efforts, focusing on showcasing the unique educational and cultural experiences they could offer. This included enhancing support services for international students, offering more scholarships tailored to Chinese students, and strengthening partnerships with Chinese educational institutions to facilitate exchange programs and ease the admission process.

This convoluted saga underscores the profound effect of geopolitics and economic tides on the ebb and flow of international students. Universities, which have started to rely heavily on the revenue generated by this demographic, find themselves on shaky ground. As the sands of global power structures continue to shift, universities are left scrambling to adapt, diversify their international student bodies, and balance their financial scales.

Universities at Crossroads: A Time to Adapt or Fade

The recruitment playbook for universities around the globe has been undergoing a quiet yet transformative revision. Universities, once reliant on a small cluster of countries, including China and India, for their international student population and corresponding revenue, are having a moment of reckoning. The precariousness of this overreliance has set off alarm bells, pushing these institutions to step back and reassess their game plan.

Emerging markets like Brazil, Nigeria, and Vietnam, teeming with young minds and rapidly expanding middle classes, have become attractive hunting grounds. Consider this: From 2016 to 2020, American universities saw a 33 percent surge in enrollment from sub-Saharan Africa, according to the Institute of International Education.[7] Or this: UK universities reported a 63 percent increase in Nigerian student numbers from 2019 to 2021, as per the UK Council for International Student Affairs.[12]

While Australian universities experienced a notable increase in Chinese student enrollments following the decline in the United States in 2018, this surge underscored a different challenge. As revealed in a 2019 paper published by the Centre for Independent Studies,[13] Australia's higher education sector found itself grappling with an overreliance on China. This dependence was particularly significant as international students, notably those from China, contribute a substantial portion of the universities' revenue. The situation highlighted the risks associated with relying too heavily on a single source country for international student enrollments.

Heeding the warning, Australian universities recalibrated their focus towards these new, promising markets. The University of Sydney, for example, saw a 50 percent bump in Vietnamese student enrollment in 2018.[14]

To stay ahead of this evolving curve, universities are doubling down on innovative recruitment measures. Some, like the University of Nottingham, are setting up shop-in recruitment hotspots with satellite campuses in China and Malaysia. Others are leveraging technology to reach students who might otherwise remain unreachable. The COVID-19 pandemic's push toward online learning demonstrated this potential. Recent data reveal a substantial increase in online course enrollments at US universities, reflecting a significant shift in educational trends. Figures from the National Centre for Education Statistics indicate a higher participation in distance education than in the pre-pandemic period, with 36 percent of undergraduate students enrolled in at least one distance education course in 2019, increasing to 75 percent in 2020.[15]

Yet, recruiting a diverse student body is only half the battle won. The real challenge lies in ensuring academic support for second-language learners and infusing a global flavor into teaching and research. The University of Melbourne, in a nod to this need, rolled out a host of language-support services and cross-cultural communication workshops in 2021.

As the fight for international students intensifies, differentiation becomes a crucial weapon. In 2018, the Massachusetts Institute of Technology (MIT) announced a significant investment in the field of computing and artificial intelligence (AI). They committed $1 billion to establish the new MIT Stephen A. Schwarzman College of Computing.[16]

Strategies for diversification are as varied as the student body universities are courting: partnerships with universities in emerging markets, presence at local education fairs, tailored marketing campaigns, and scholarships to sweeten the deal. The potential of online education and remote learning technologies plays a crucial role in providing educational opportunities to students for whom the costs of overseas travel are prohibitive. These technologies offer an accessible alternative, enabling a broader range of students to engage in international learning experiences without the financial burden of travel and living abroad.

Thriving in this shifting landscape requires universities to keep a keen eye on global economic and demographic trends and remain alert to changes in immigration policies. This might involve pouring resources into market research to sniff out new opportunities, establishing ties with businesses and governments in emerging markets, or offering multilingual courses.

Furthermore, universities need to differentiate themselves – whether through unique research programs, state-of-the-art facilities, or robust alumni networks. As Sir Steve Smith, vice-chancellor of the University of Exeter, observed, "Universities will need to adapt or die. There is no safe harbor." These aren't just wise words. In the volatile arena of global higher education, they're the harsh reality. Adaptability, foresight, and strategic diversification aren't just assets anymore – they're a matter of survival.

The Next Act: A Futuristic Gaze into Higher Education

As we progress deeper into the twenty-first century, the arena of international higher education is poised for transformation. The forces at play are many – the ebb and flow of global economies, the unpredictability of geopolitics, relentless technological progress, and ever-changing demographics. Each of these elements promises to etch its impact on the future contours of global universities.

One of the primary anticipated changes involves a transformation in student recruitment strategies. Diversification is expected to replace dependence. Universities are likely to loosen their dependence on traditional international student powerhouses like China and India. Instead, they're set to pump resources into wooing potential students in emerging markets. Countries like Nigeria, Vietnam, and Brazil, riding high on growing middle classes and young populations, are primed to become hotspots for international student recruitment.

The lessons from the COVID-19 pandemic, particularly the move to online learning, have not been lost on universities. This unexpected foray into the virtual world broadened their reach, offering education to international students hemmed in by travel restrictions. Expect this trend to stick around, with universities supplementing traditional teaching with digital innovation.

As the student body becomes a melting pot of diverse cultures, universities will have to ensure their curriculum keeps pace. An integration of global perspectives in teaching and research will likely become the norm, and multilingual courses could become commonplace. Additionally, universities could increase academic support for those grappling with a second language. To set themselves apart in a fiercely competitive market, they might turn to unique research programs and cutting-edge facilities.

Universities standing on the cusp of this evolution must be defined by adaptability, foresight, and strategic diversification. Navigating this shifting landscape successfully will require a fine-tuned understanding of global trends and the readiness to switch methods when required. Balancing the expansion of student populations for revenue growth, without diluting the quality of education, will be a delicate and complex endeavor.

The future, while strewn with challenges, is also rife with opportunities. It promises an era of growth, evolution, and expansion of intellectual frontiers. However, this journey demands resilience, a knack for innovation, and a readiness to adapt relentlessly. The guiding light for universities navigating these shifts should always remain their raison d'etre – offering top-notch education while nurturing a diverse, inclusive, and globally conscious student community.

In the words of Albert Einstein, "The measure of intelligence is the ability to change." The unfolding scenario in higher education will test universities on this very premise. It's not merely their capacity to impart knowledge or inspire students that will mark their intelligence, but rather their resilience and agility in adapting to change. This means reevaluating and potentially overhauling long-standing educational models and pedagogies to be more aligned with the needs of a rapidly evolving world. Universities must demonstrate their ability to not just survive but to thrive amid transformation. This requires a proactive stance in embracing new technologies, forging innovative partnerships, and revising curricula to include skills that are relevant in the modern job market. In doing so, they can evolve from traditional centers of learning to dynamic hubs of innovation, better equipped to prepare students for an unpredictable future.

References

1 "State Higher Education on Funding Cuts Have Pushed Costs to Students, Worsened Inequality," accessed July 29, 2023, https://www.cbpp.org/research/state-budget-and-tax/state-higher-education-funding-cuts-have-pushed-costs-to-students#_ftnref1.
2 "Historical Inflation Rates: 1914–2023," accessed December 16, 2023, https://www.usinflationcalculator.com/inflation/historical-inflation-rates/.
3 "EUA Public Funding Observatory," *European University Association*, 2015, accessed May 5, 2024, https://eua.eu/resources/projects/586-public-funding-observatory.html.
4 "11+ Education Cost Statistics in Singapore (2023)," accessed July 29, 2023, https://smartwealth.sg/education-cost-statistics-singapore/.
5 C. Fan, S. H. Law, S. Ibrahim, and N. A. M. Naseem (2022). "The New Economic Era Analysis of the Structure System of Chinese Household Consumption Expenditure Based on the ELES Model," *Computational Intelligence and Neuroscience*, 2022, 3278194.
6 D. Farrell, U. A. Gersch, and E. Stephenson (2006). "The Value of China's Emerging Middle Class," *McKinsey Quarterly*, 2(I), 60.
7 "International Students Data," accessed July 29, 2023, https://opendoorsdata.org/annual-release/international-students/.
8 "New NAFSA Data Reveal International Student Economic Contributions Continue to Rebound," *Association of International Educators*, accessed July 29, 2023, https://www.nafsa.org/about/about-nafsa/new-nafsa-data-reveal-international-student-economic-contributions-continue.

9 "Chinese Students in US Seen as Vital Link," *China Daily*, accessed December 16, 2023, https://global.chinadaily.com.cn/a/202312/07/WS6571dc78a31090682a5f2079.html.
10 "International Students in Canada Continue to Grow in 2019," accessed July 29, 2023, https://cbie.ca/international-students-in-canada-continue-to-grow-in-2019/.
11 "Higher Education Statistics—Student Data," accessed July 29, 2023, https://www.education.gov.au/higher-education-statistics/student-data.
12 "International Facts and Figures 2022," accessed July 29, 2023, https://www.universitiesuk.ac.uk/universities-uk-international/insights-and-publications/uuki-publications/international-facts-and-figures-2022.
13 S. J. Babones (2019). "The China Student Boom and the Risks It Poses to Australian Universities," *The Centre for Independent Studies*, accessed May 19, 2024, https://www.cis.org.au/publication/the-china-student-boom-and-the-risks-it-poses-to-australian-universities/.
14 "Sydney Accepting the Best Students from Vietnam," accessed July 29, 2023, https://www.sydney.edu.au/news-opinion/news/2018/01/29/-sydney-accepting-the-best-students-from-vietnam.html.
15 "Distance Learning," *National Centre for Education Statistics*, accessed December 16, 2023, https://nces.ed.gov/fastfacts/display.asp?id=80.
16 "MIT to Launch $1 Billion New College of Computing," *MIT CSAIL*, accessed December 16, 2023, https://www.csail.mit.edu/news/mit-launch-1-billion-new-college-computing.

3 The Great Divide

Unmasking the Mismatch

The roots of this divergence can largely be traced back to the speed at which technological change is transforming the world of work. Universities, with their often archaic curricula, are training students for a job market that no longer exists. They're preparing young minds for a race while the finish line keeps shifting.

The World Economic Forum's 2020 "Future of Jobs Report" paints a stark picture of this reality. It warns that by 2025, humans and machines will be sharing the workload equally.[1] This tectonic shift is a result of rapid strides in automation, artificial intelligence, and machine learning, which are reshaping industries and job profiles.

Society's perception of work is also in flux. The gig economy is no longer the exception but increasingly the norm. A report by the Mastercard Center for Inclusive Growth shows that gig work in the Asia-Pacific Region has ballooned by 20 percent annually over the last half-decade.[2] This shift has led to an increased demand for skills such as digital literacy, entrepreneurship, and self-management – areas that traditional university curricula often overlook.

LinkedIn's 2022 Workforce Report further highlighted this mismatch. While employers are hunting for soft skills like emotional intelligence, communication, and problem-solving, academia continues to emphasize hard, subject-specific skills.[3]

Geographic constraints are a significant obstacle. Many universities, deeply rooted in and influenced by their local cultures, find themselves struggling to equip students for a globalized job market. This issue was highlighted in a 2021 survey by the Institute of International Education,[4] which found that approximately three-quarters of students aim for careers with an international scope. These aspirations, however, may not be fully supported by their current educational experiences, which are often more aligned with local rather than global contexts.

The mismatch is glaring in the technology sector, one of the world's fastest-growing industries. As per *Code.org*, there were over 1,400,000 open

DOI: 10.4324/9781003476504-4

computing jobs in the United States in 2020, but only 400,000 computer science students graduated into the workforce that year.[5] The yawning gap underscores the failure of the education system to keep up with the demands of the job market.

Universities are waking up to these challenges. They're trying to bridge the gap, and while they are not stuck in the Dark Ages, altering their long-established models of education is akin to turning a supertanker – it's slow and complex and requires a carefully planned route. Many universities have already made significant strides, integrating digital technologies into their curricula, adopting more flexible learning models and fostering interdisciplinary research. However, the pace of technological advancement and changing societal needs still pose a significant challenge. Changes are needed at every level – from curriculum design to teaching methodologies, faculty development, evaluation systems, and the deeply ingrained culture of academic institutions. Overcoming these obstacles requires strategic foresight, resources, and a willingness to shake off the comfort of the familiar, continuing the progress already made while accelerating the transformation to meet the demands of the twenty-first century.

New Market, New Rules: Technology, Globalization, and Societal Shifts

Technology, especially automation and artificial intelligence, is changing the employment landscape at breakneck speed. As per a Brookings Institution report from 2019, about 25 percent of jobs in the United States are at high risk of automation.[6] The World Economic Forum has similarly predicted that by 2025, machines will take over more of our current tasks than humans. Jobs are disappearing, but new ones are springing up, demanding skills that were unheard of just a few years ago. Today, roles such as data scientists and AI specialists are among the fastest growing in the job market.[1]

Globalization, meanwhile, has been making the world a smaller place, leading to more interconnected economies and societies. According to the report from Statista, global trade has ballooned by 370 percent from 1990 to 2015.[7] As a result, employees are increasingly working across different cultures and time zones, requiring a greater understanding of diverse cultures and languages.

However, globalization is not a one-way street. The recent US-China trade war, for example, triggered a significant realignment of global supply chains. Many multinational corporations are now reducing their dependence on a single country for critical resources. This so-called ally-shoring phenomenon involves diversifying supply chains among countries that share similar values and norms. The trend has been exacerbated by the COVID-19 pandemic, which laid bare the vulnerability of consolidated supply chains. As reported by Boston Consulting Group in a previous study, it was anticipated that by the year 2023, North American and European companies would redirect $1 trillion in global trade flows toward regional countries, dramatically reshaping the geography of supply chains.[8]

These shifts demand a new skillset from graduates. Universities will need to prepare students for the evolving landscape of global trade, teaching them about the regulations, business practices, and cultures of "ally" countries. Furthermore, as companies aim to reduce their carbon footprint in response to growing demands for sustainability, skills related to green supply chain management will become increasingly valuable.

Society itself is undergoing a transformation, changing the nature of work. There's an increased focus on sustainability, social impact, and mental health. The 2021 Deloitte Global Millennial Survey found that a significant majority of millennials and Gen Zs believe businesses should focus more on societal challenges and less on profit. Meanwhile, a Qualtrics survey showed that the pandemic had a detrimental impact on the mental health of 42 percent of respondents.[9]

Against this backdrop, universities face the Herculean task of revamping their curricula to meet these new demands. They'll need to balance disciplinary depth with a broader understanding of global trends and teach skills that remain relevant amid rapid technological, geopolitical, and societal shifts. It's a daunting challenge, but as the saying goes, "In the midst of chaos, there is also opportunity."

What Employers Really Want

The evolving workforce has spawned an arms race between universities and the job market – a fight to equip students with an armor of skills suitable for the new world. In this epoch, skills are like moving targets, metamorphosing in line with technological advances and employer demands. Yet, the dichotomy between hard skills and soft skills, two distinct species in the skills ecosystem, remains intact.

Hard skills are akin to solid, quantifiable bricks – skills that can be taught, practiced, and measured, such as coding or data analysis. These are the cornerstones of traditional education, the badge of a university graduate. Then, there are soft skills, elusive yet critical in the modern workplace. These are the subtler, often intangible skills that influence how one interacts, solves problems, and adapts to change. Soft skills, ranging from creativity and persuasion to adaptability and emotional intelligence, are the necessary complement to hard skills. In today's dynamic work environment, soft skills are just as vital as hard skills. They enable individuals to navigate complex social environments, foster effective teamwork, and adapt to rapidly changing job requirements. In industries increasingly driven by teamwork and innovation, the ability to communicate, lead, and empathize is often what differentiates a good employee from a great one, making soft skills essential for both personal and organizational success.

A LinkedIn pulse check in 2020 revealed an increasing thirst for soft skills among employers. Technology, for all its monumental advances, has yet to replicate human creativity, making it a valuable currency in the job market.[10] An Adobe report backed this claim, stating that businesses nurturing creativity were rewarded with an 85 percent boost in productivity. However, job seekers lacking in soft skills face significant challenges in this landscape. They may struggle with effective communication, teamwork, and problem-solving in workplace settings, which can hinder their career advancement and limit their opportunities. In a market that increasingly values these interpersonal and creative competencies, the absence of soft skills can be a critical drawback, often leading to difficulties in securing and retaining employment in roles that demand high levels of collaboration and adaptability.

The hard skills narrative has a distinct tech flavor. As per the same LinkedIn study, the most sought-after hard skills marketplace were blockchain, cloud computing, analytical reasoning, artificial intelligence, and UX design. This trend mirrors the findings of the World Economic Forum, which spotlighted roles like data analysts and AI specialists as the fastest growing in the job market.

Yet, this cry for tech skills echoes unanswered in the cavernous skills gap. IBM's 2020 skills study painted a stark picture, revealing that 59 percent of companies were scrambling to find employees versed in data science and analytics. A Burning Glass Technologies study added another dimension, recording a 118 percent surge in AI-related job postings over five years.[11]

But what are universities doing? Their response has been glacial, with many institutes dawdling in updating their curriculum. The result? A chasm between graduates' skillsets and the demands of employers, a void deepening with every passing day.

However, beneath this high-stakes duel between hard and soft skills lurks a dark horse in the skills race – *grit*. Grit is the intangible force of determination, the unwavering passion to pursue long-term goals and the resilience to soldier on in the face of adversity. Thanks to the pioneering work of psychologist Angela Duckworth, her research on grit has significant implications for employers, emphasizing the importance of perseverance and passion for long-term goals in the workplace. Her findings suggest that grit, rather than just intelligence or talent, is a critical predictor of success. This insight has led employers to value and seek out grit in potential hires, recognizing that individuals who demonstrate resilience and sustained commitment are often more effective and successful in their roles, especially in challenging work environments.[12]

Teaching grit, however, is no mean feat for universities. Unlike the teachable hard skills or soft skills, which can be nurtured through team projects or discussions, grit is a combination of personal experiences and mindset.

Universities, with their well-defined paths and guidance, often don't provide the raw material – challenges and setbacks – required to build grit.

Real-world problem-solving, internships, entrepreneurial projects, and experiential learning may be the antidotes, providing opportunities for students to stumble, fall, and learn to get up again. But this is not just a matter of tweaking the curriculum; it's about a cultural upheaval in academia, about prioritizing resilience and problem-solving over the traditional gold stars of grades and degrees.

It's a treacherous path strewn with complex challenges, but universities must navigate to keep their graduates relevant in a turbulent job market. They must foster grit, not just knowledge, to equip their students with the tenacity to weather the storms of the future workplace.

The World's Unhealthy Fixation on Traditional Disciplines

From Shanghai to San Francisco, a shared obsession echoes in classrooms, parent-teacher meetings, and university corridors. It's an obsession that transcends borders, a universal fixation on a handful of traditional, esteemed fields – medicine, law, engineering. This collective fascination, steeped in prestige and perceived stability, is creating a seismic rift between the skills taught by universities and the evolving demands of the job market.

In Asia, for instance, the grip of certain disciplines is particularly tight. There, fields like medicine, engineering, and computer science are worshipped and placed high on the altar of societal prestige.

A recent survey conducted by Mindler,[13] an online career-counseling platform, revealed a concerning trend among Indian students regarding their career awareness. The survey, which involved 10,000 participants aged fourteen to twenty-one from across India, found that a remarkable 93 percent of the students were aware of only seven career options. These options include law, engineering, medicine, accounts and finance, design, computer applications and IT, and management. This limited awareness is in stark contrast to the 250 different career options available in India. Yet, this reverential focus often blinds them to the burgeoning fields that hold the keys to the future, such as data analytics, environmental science, and digital marketing.

The Middle East and North Africa tell a similar tale, with medicine and engineering being the twin lodestars for students. However, this narrow focus churns out an oversupply of graduates, flooding the job market and creating a legion of unemployed degree holders. The World Bank's statistics underscore the severity; countries like Tunisia and Jordan report higher unemployment rates among university graduates than those with less education.[14]

Meanwhile, in the United States and Europe, the pendulum swings toward business-related degrees. The Association to Advance Collegiate Schools of

Business reported a notable figure: there were over 250,000 MBA enrollments worldwide in the 2020–21 academic year.[15] While business acumen is undeniably valuable, this dominant narrative often obscures the equally vital need for technical skills in this digital era and the softer, yet essential skills of creativity, empathy, and cross-cultural competency.

This worldwide infatuation with a narrow selection of disciplines is setting the stage for a supply-demand imbalance in the job market. Universities are churning out a deluge of graduates, armed with degrees that are increasingly out of sync with the skills sought by employers. The result? A wave of underemployed graduates on one end and a gaping skills deficit in emerging fields on the other.

The remedy to this global challenge lies in a collective shift in mindset among parents, students, and educational institutions. They must move beyond traditional notions of education and career success, embracing the reality that the job market and the skills it demands are evolving rapidly. In this era of continuous change, recognizing and adapting to the expanding and varied landscape of opportunities is crucial. Only through this adaptive mindset can we realign the goals of academia with the needs of the job market, effectively preparing students for the challenges and opportunities of the future.

The University Conundrum: Racing Against the Clock of Relevance

In the race against obsolescence, universities around the globe are facing a critical challenge. Their primary mission is to bridge the skills gap, ensuring that students are adequately prepared for the demands of the modern workforce. However, this task is becoming increasingly complex as the requirements of the job market continue to evolve at a rapid pace. Universities must constantly update their curricula and teaching methods to keep pace with these changes, ensuring that their graduates remain competitive and relevant in an ever-changing employment landscape.

The first challenge comes from the notable pace at which industries are morphing. The World Economic Forum sounded the alarm in a 2020 report: by 2025, half of all employees will need reskilling, a side effect of the skyrocketing adoption of technology.[1] Deloitte chimed in with a startling fact in 2020 – the half-life of learned skills has shrunk to a mere five years.[16] This ticking clock means the knowledge students acquire during their first years of university may already be collecting dust by the time they done their graduation caps.

Universities, often resembling mammoth ships that are slow to change course, grapple with updating their curricula to match these breakneck changes. Curricular reform in educational institutions tends to progress at a sluggish pace, often taking years even under optimal conditions. This bureaucratic inertia results in graduates entering the workforce with skills that are not aligned with the current demands of the industry.

The second hurdle in the race arises from the ever-diversifying skill sets required by today's employers. The World Economic Forum, in its "Future of Jobs Report," has singled out skills such as complex problem-solving, critical thinking, and creativity as integral for modern work.[17] Yet, universities often find themselves in a labyrinth trying to infuse these expansive skill sets into a single program of study. The reason? A historic hangover – the deeply ingrained disciplinary structure of higher education that often acts as a barrier to cross-disciplinary learning.

Adding to the challenges faced by educational institutions is the rising demand for digital skills among new graduates. This need exposes another chink in the universities' armor – the struggle of traditional programs to equip students with the necessary digital skills for effective problem-solving, innovation, and adaptation in a rapidly evolving digital economy.

Then, as if the race wasn't daunting enough, along came COVID-19. The pandemic forced a seismic shift to remote learning, leaving universities scrambling to replicate hands-on, practical training in a virtual world. This situation revealed the struggle to provide practical, hands-on training in a digital format, underscoring the existing need for improvement in digital education and readiness within these institutions. The rapid transition highlighted the considerable hurdles that lay ahead in adapting educational models to meet the demands of an increasingly digital world.

Universities, now more than ever, are recognizing the need to evolve beyond traditional educational models. This evolution involves not just a superficial update of curricula but a deeper, systemic transformation. They are exploring innovative approaches such as integrating real-world problem-solving into academic programs, fostering closer collaborations with industry leaders for practical insights, and emphasizing interdisciplinary studies that mirror the complex nature of today's global challenges. These steps are crucial for equipping students not just with knowledge, but with the adaptability and critical-thinking skills necessary to navigate and succeed in a rapidly changing professional environment.

Innovation at the Helm: Universities Plotting the Course of Adaptation

Universities around the world are actively adapting to change by implementing innovative strategies. Key elements of these strategies include revamping their curricula to be more relevant to today's world, integrating experiential learning to enhance practical understanding, and increasing the use of technology to enrich the educational experience. These efforts are essential to ensure that higher education remains effective and responsive to the evolving needs of students and the job market.

Take Northeastern University in Boston. Long a champion of the cooperative education model, the university has been weaving traditional classroom study with real-world work experience. The fruit of this novel approach? A significant percentage (97 percent) of Northeastern graduates are employed or enrolled in graduate school within nine months of graduation in 2022, a testament to the effectiveness of the co-op program.[18]

Following suit is Canada's University of Waterloo, renowned for its potent co-op programs. The numbers tell a compelling tale – a 96.4 percent employment rate for Waterloo's co-op students post-graduation, according to a 2019 report by the Higher Education Quality Council of Ontario. The figure overshadows the provincial average of 87.6 percent, underlining the impact of their strategy.[19]

Beyond the borders of the conventional classroom, universities are injecting technology into the bloodstream of education. Stanford University and MIT, leading the charge, have launched online learning platforms Coursera and edX, vaulting education into cyberspace. These platforms, per a 2022 report by Class Central, have become the virtual classrooms of over 70 million and 34 million learners worldwide, respectively.[20] The heavy focus on in-demand skills like data science, artificial intelligence, and cloud computing signals a nod to the dynamic landscape of employable skills.

The COVID-19 pandemic led to a significant shift in educational practices, with many schools transitioning to remote or hybrid models. This change resulted in an increased reliance on online learning platforms to facilitate education outside the traditional classroom setting. The move toward these digital solutions became a key aspect of maintaining continuity in education during this period.

An intriguing development has been the budding partnerships between universities and industries. By rubbing shoulders with the corporate world, universities are ensuring they keep their fingers on the pulse of the ever-changing job market. A prime example is the collaboration between Arizona State University and technology behemoth Salesforce. In a 2022 report by *ASU News*,[21] the partners unveiled their joint venture – an education-skills mapping system, which focuses on bridging the digital skills gap. ASU, as a Salesforce Authorized Training Provider, integrates platform-centric digital skills into its curriculum, leveraging Trailhead Academy's workforce development infrastructure. This collaboration aims to address the rapidly growing demand for digital skills, expected to rise by over 50 percent by 2025. Through this partnership, ASU can provide students with up-to-date Salesforce training, certification, and validation of their digital competencies, preparing them effectively for the future workforce.

So, as the landscape of higher education twists and turns, universities are not only keeping pace but setting the course. The challenges they face are substantial, and the solutions are not less diverse. But what shines through is the indomitable spirit of innovation, a testament to the sector's unwavering commitment to arm students with the skills they need to conquer the modern workforce.

Charting the Future: From Predictions to Preparations

As we march further into the twenty-first century, the job market is akin to a chameleon, constantly changing its colors. Propelling this evolution are forces like technological advancement, globalization, climate change, and now the lingering impacts of the COVID-19 pandemic. The horizon offers not a halt but a hastening of these trends.

Technology, primarily automation and AI, is primed to continue molding the professional landscape. The World Economic Forum, in its 2020 report, painted a stark picture. By 2025, automation and AI could displace 85 million jobs. However, the same forces are also set to create 97 million new roles. These positions, likely to be technology focused, will require a mix of digital skills and human traits, such as creativity, emotional intelligence, and critical thinking.[1] While the spotlight intensifies on STEM graduates and experts in AI, machine learning, data science, and related fields, it's important to recognize that not all these new jobs will require traditional university degrees. Alternative educational pathways like vocational training, online courses, and industry certifications will play a crucial role in reskilling and upskilling the existing workforce, providing opportunities for those affected by job displacement to adapt and thrive in this new landscape.

Meanwhile, the labor market's globalization is set to surge, with remote work eroding geographic boundaries. The COVID-19 pandemic fast-tracked this shift, with many organizations now considering remote work as a long-haul strategy. This shift could dramatically redefine job prospects, throwing open global opportunities for graduates, but also igniting fiercer competition.

Climate change, the elephant in the room, isn't just a crisis but a catalyst for "green jobs." As economies lean toward sustainability, the International Renewable Energy Agency estimates that the renewable energy sector could generate 42 million jobs globally by 2050. Fields like environmental science, sustainability, and clean-energy technology are on the cusp of explosive growth.[22]

While these changes offer opportunities, they also present challenges. They run the risk of widening the "skills gap" – the divide between the skills job-seekers bring to the table and what employers are actually scouting for. Worse still, they could fuel inequality if access to necessary education and training is uneven.

To ready their students for this imminent future, universities will need to pivot, spotlighting interdisciplinary education, soft skills, digital aptitude, and lifelong learning. Building bridges with the industry could also ensure the education on offer stays tuned to the job market's changing frequency.

In conclusion, while the future job market might bristle with challenges, it also brims with opportunities. By proactively adjusting and equipping students for tomorrow's jobs, universities can help temper potential issues and foster a more inclusive, dynamic, and robust job market.

References

1 "The Future of Jobs Report 2020," accessed July 30, 2023, https://weforum.org/reports/the-future-of-jobs-report-2020/.
2 "Fueling the Global Gig Economy," accessed July 30, 2023, https://www.mastercard.us/content/dam/public/mastercardcom/na/us/en/documents/mastercard-fueling-the-global-gig-economy-2020.pdf.
3 "LinkedIn 2022 Workforce Diversity Report," accessed July 30, 2023, https://news.linkedin.com/en-us/2022/october/2022-workforce-diversity-report.
4 "IIE Survey: Universities Indicate Optimism, Confidence on International Educational Exchange," *Institute of International Education*, accessed December 16, 2023, https://www.iie.org/news/iie-survey-universities-indicate-optimism-confidence-on-international-educational-exchange/.
5 "Every Student in Every School Should Have the Opportunity to Learn Computer Science," accessed July 30, 2023, https://code.org/files/Code.orgOverview.pdf.
6 M. Muro, R. Maxim, and J. Whiton (2019). "Automation and Artificial Intelligence: How Machines Are Affecting People and Places," *The Brookings Metropolitan Policy Program*, accessed May 19, 2024, https://www.brookings.edu/articles/automation-and-artificial-intelligence-how-machines-affect-people-and-places/#:~:text=Almost%20no%20occupation%20will%20be,of%20their%20tasks%20potentially%20automatable.
7 "Worldwide Export Volume in the Trade Since 1950," *Statista*, accessed December 30, https://www.statista.com/statistics/264682/worldwide-export-volume-in-the-trade-since-1950/.
8 "Protectionism, Pandemic, War, and the Future of Trade," accessed July 30, 2023, https://www.bcg.com/publications/2023/protectionism-pandemic-war-and-future-of-trade.
9 "The Other COVID-19 Crisis: Mental Health," accessed July 30, 2023, https://www.qualtrics.com/blog/confronting-mental-health/.
10 "The Most In-Demand Soft Skills of 2020," accessed July 30, 2023, https://www.linkedin.com/pulse/most-in-demand-soft-skills-2020-saba-usman/.
11 "IBM Predicts Demand For Data Scientists Will Soar 28% by 2020," accessed July 30, 2023, https://www.forbes.com/sites/louiscolumbus/2017/05/13/ibm-predicts-demand-for-data-scientists-will-soar-28-by-2020/?sh=2378d8bc7e3b.
12 C. S. Dweck, *Mindset: The New Psychology of Success* (New York: Ballantine, 2006).
13 "93 Percent Indian Students Aware of Just Seven Career Options: What Are Parents Doing Wrong?" *India Today*, accessed December 16, 2023, https://www.indiatoday.in/education-today/news/story/93-indian-students-aware-of-just-seven-career-options-what-are-parents-doing-wrong-1446205-2019-02-04.
14 "A New Era of Work in the Middle East and North Africa: What Is to Be Done?" *The World Bank*, accessed December 30, https://blogs.worldbank.org/jobs/new-era-work-middle-east-and-north-africa-what-be-done.
15 "How Many Students Are Studying for an MBA?" *Poets&Quants*, accessed December 30, https://poetsandquants.com/2022/04/29/how-many-students-are-studying-for-an-mba/.
16 "Closing the Employability Skills Gap," *Deloitte Insight*, accessed December 16, 2023, https://www2.deloitte.com/us/en/insights/focus/technology-and-the-future-of-work/closing-the-employability-skills-gap.html.
17 "The Future of Jobs Report 2020," *World Economic Forum*, accessed December 16, 2023, https://www.weforum.org/publications/the-future-of-jobs-report-2020.
18 "Career Outcomes," *Northeastern University*, accessed December 16, 2023, https://careeroutcomes.northeastern.edu/.

19 "2019 Co-Operative Education Annual Report," accessed July 30, 2023, https://uwaterloo.ca/associate-provost-co-operative-and-experiential-education/sites/default/files/uploads/documents/2019-co-op-annual-report.pdf.
20 "2022 Year in Review: The 'New Normal' That Wasn't," accessed July 30, 2023, https://www.classcentral.com/report/2022-year-in-review/.
21 "ASU, Salesforce's Trailhead Academy Join Forces to Close the Digital Skills Gap," *ASU News*, accessed December 16, 2023, https://news.asu.edu/20220502-asu-and-salesforces-trailhead-academy-join-forces-close-digital-skills-gap.
22 "Sustainability Jobs: 42 Million Renewable Energy Jobs by 2050," accessed July 30, 2023, https://www.linkedin.com/pulse/sustainability-jobs-42-million-renewable-energy-2050-chhantyal/.

4 The High Price of Higher Learning

Navigating the Financial Quagmire

The ascent of the cost of higher education has been a concerning trajectory observed across decades. But this isn't just about the dollars and cents stretching thin for students and their families. It threatens to shackle social mobility, widen the chasm of inequality, and fester into a full-blown student debt crisis.

The United States offers a glaring spotlight on this phenomenon. The College Board's data sketch a stark contrast: a private nonprofit four-year institution demanded an average tuition fee of about $15,160 (adjusted for inflation) for the academic year 1980–81. Fast forward to the 2020–21 academic year, the figure spiraled to a substantial $37,650. This tuition turmoil amounts to a 150 percent increase in cost.[1]

Across the Atlantic, in the United Kingdom, the cost of higher education hasn't been immune to this inflationary trend. The turn of 2012 marked a watershed moment in the UK's higher education financing. Universities got the green signal to pump up tuition fees to £9,000 annually for domestic and EU students – a number that now hovers at £9,250. That's a significant leap from the earlier £3,000-a-year cap in 2006 and signifies a tangible shift in higher education's financial responsibility, moving from the state's purse to individual pockets.[2]

Several elements have stoked this rise in cost. One element is the uptick in operational expenses, including faculty paychecks and administrative overheads. A 2020 study in the *Journal of Higher Education Policy and Management* pinpoints a 61 percent climb in administrative costs at US universities between 1993 and 2007.[3]

Meanwhile, the race for "amenities" has added fuel to the fire. Universities, particularly in the United States, are splurging on grandeur – from state-of-the-art sports facilities to opulent dorms – in a bid to reel in students. A 2023 research piece in the *Economics of Education Review* found a correlation: US public universities that spent more on amenities saw a surge in both the quantity and quality of applicants.[4]

But there's more to this cost conundrum. The global financial crisis of 2008 triggered a cutback in state funding for public universities, and students ended up shouldering the financial load. A report by the Center on Budget and Policy Priorities disclosed a startling statistic: by 2018, public investment in two- and four-year colleges was still languishing at more than $6.6 billion below its 2008 benchmark.[5]

The ripple effects of these cost escalations are far reaching. Students are saddled up with increasing debt loads to foot their education bills. The Federal Reserve Bank of New York revealed a significant number in 2021: student loan debt in the United States had ballooned to a mammoth $1.7 trillion, ensnaring about 43 million Americans in its grip.[6]

These skyrocketing costs are also casting shadows on access to education and widening socioeconomic fault lines. A 2023 research paper by the *American Economics Review* underscored that steeper tuition fees can deter enrollment, particularly among less affluent students, diminishing the socioeconomic diversity on campuses.[7]

Universities, in their quest to tackle these challenges, are testing the waters with alternative funding avenues, such as income share agreements (ISAs), which commit students to pay a slice of their future earnings to cover tuition fees. The rallying cry for tuition-free or debt-free public higher education has also grown louder. In 2014, Germany took a bold leap, scrapping tuition fees for undergraduate students at all public universities.[8] This policy change led to an increase in student enrollment, including a rise in international students attracted by the prospect of free education. However, it also brought challenges such as strained resources and overcrowded classrooms at universities.

But these measures merely skim the surface, failing to tackle the roots of the cost explosion. Thus, a sweeping reform of higher education funding is called for, one that blends policy changes and institutional accountability. This reform aims to slam the brakes on the runaway growth in tuition fees and ensure that higher education remains within everyone's reach.

The Cost Labyrinth: Navigating the Causes of Tuition Inflation

Inflating tuition fees present a convoluted challenge, woven into a tapestry of factors with overlapping threads and murky connections.

One significant challenge facing higher education is the steady reduction of public funding. In the United States, there was a notable decrease of 16 percent in state funding for public colleges between 2008 and 2017, as reported by the State Higher Education Executive Officers Association.[9] This decline, coupled with financial crises and fiscal austerity measures, has resulted in reduced government support for universities. Faced with these financial constraints, institutions have increasingly had to rely on raising tuition fees to cover their operational costs, directly impacting students with higher educational expenses.

Simultaneously, operational costs within universities have shot up. It's not just about paying the faculty anymore. Campus maintenance, administrative expenses, and student services pile up, adding weight to the expenditure scales. *A Journal of Education Finance* study revealed a remarkable statistic: between 1993 and 2007, administrative spending at US universities ballooned by 61 percent, outgrowing even the expenditure on instruction.[10]

Meanwhile, universities are feeling the heat to go beyond the chalk-and-talk teaching approach. While it's true that many are enhancing their appeal through investments in student amenities, such as modern sports facilities and upgraded living and dining options, the implications of this trend extend beyond mere surface-level appeal. These investments, while attractive, raise critical questions about the shifting priorities in higher education funding. A 2020 McKinsey report found that US public universities increasing their spending on amenities attracted more and higher-quality applicants.[11] However, this strategy also leads to a complex debate about the balance between enhancing student experience and maintaining educational affordability, as these high-cost amenities can contribute to rising tuition fees, potentially impacting accessibility and student debt.

The soaring demand for higher education adds another layer of complexity. As the job market increasingly calls for a degree, the thirst for higher education intensifies. According to a US Bureau of Labor Statistics report, occupations demanding a master's degree will see 16.7 percent growth from 2016 to 2026 – the fastest among all educational levels.[12] This demand surge essentially grants universities the leverage to hike their prices.

The tangled web of tuition escalation also ensnares student loans. Born out of the noble intention of making education accessible to all, these loans have inadvertently poured fuel on the tuition fire. Easy access to student loans has expanded the pool of students who can shoulder higher tuition, thereby indirectly enabling universities to inflate their fees.

Untangling this tuition cost conundrum, then, requires a deep dive into these myriad intertwined causes. The road to resolution might be paved with policy interventions, university spending reforms, and a drastic reshaping of the higher education business model. The words of the late Nelson Mandela ring true: "Education is the most powerful weapon which you can use to change the world." It's time we ensure this potent weapon doesn't extract an insurmountable price.

The Domino Effect: Student Debt and Deepening Inequality

The continuous rise in higher education costs has had a significant impact, leading to an increase in student debt, particularly in the United States.

According to the US Federal Reserve data from 2021, about 45 million borrowers are dealing with a total of approximately $1.7 trillion in student loan debt. This amount represents an increase of over 100 percent compared to a decade earlier, making student loan debt the second-largest category of consumer debt in the United States, surpassed only by mortgage debt.[6]

These swelling debt numbers cast long shadows over individuals and society alike. A *National Bureau of Economic Research* study threw light on the deterrent effect of sky-high tuition fees and the accompanying debt burden. The looming specter of crippling debt often scares off potential students, particularly those from lower-income backgrounds. Consequently, these individuals may choose to steer clear of higher education altogether – a decision that can limit their career trajectories and earning capabilities.[13]

Those who brave the debt path to fund their education often find themselves grappling with intense financial strain after they graduate. According to a survey by the OneWisconsin Institute, American borrowers take an average of 21.1 years to clear their debts for a bachelor's degree.[14] This prolonged debt-repayment phase can hinder major life milestones, such as buying a home, starting a family, or even stashing away savings for retirement.

Additionally, the skyrocketing cost of higher education sharpens the edges of socioeconomic inequality. Even though scholarships, grants, and financial aid provide some respite, they often fail to cover the full cost of education. Students from lower-income backgrounds tend to enroll in less selective colleges than their academic abilities would permit, often due to financial constraints. This trend of undermatching can restrict their educational and career potential, thereby contributing to the continuous cycle of inequality.

In the United Kingdom, the situation mirrors the problem in the United States. A report by the Institute for Fiscal Studies revealed a harsh reality – students from the poorest 40 percent of families in the UK were saddled with an average debt of £57,000 ($74,000) upon graduation in 2017.[15] This fact widens the economic chasm between the rich and the poor even further. While wealthier families may also take out student loans, they often have more resources to contribute toward education costs, potentially reducing the amount borrowed or enabling faster repayment. This disparity contributes to widening the economic gap between rich and poor, as those from lower-income backgrounds are more likely to start their postgraduation lives with a higher debt load.

The task of tackling these burgeoning issues falls upon the collective shoulders of policymakers, educational institutions, and society as a whole. Novel approaches such as income-share agreements – where students repay a percentage of their postgraduation income – may form part of the solution, along with an enhanced emphasis on vocational education and training. What remains clear, though, is the unsustainability of the current trajectory of higher education costs – an issue that screams for urgent attention. Echoing the words of Robert F. Kennedy, "Each time a man stands up for an ideal, or acts to improve the lot of others, he sends forth a tiny ripple of hope." It's high time that higher education sparked such hopeful ripples, rather than waves of debilitating debt.

Under the Microscope: Dissecting the Cost Conundrum

When it comes to the ballooning costs of higher education, various investigative tools and models come into play to demystify the issue – chief among them being regression analysis, surveys and longitudinal studies, and economic models.

Regression analysis often becomes the scalpel in the hands of researchers, slicing through the complex relationships between state funding, institutional expenditures, and tuition costs. For instance, a study published in the *Journal of Economic Perspectives* in 2012 revealed a stark truth: a rise in spending on instruction and academic support significantly influences tuition prices at public four-year institutions.[16] This type of intricate analysis becomes a compass, guiding policy decisions and steering institutional practices.

Then we have the role of surveys and longitudinal studies – two key instruments that shed light on the repercussions of soaring tuition costs and burgeoning student debt on individuals and society. The U.S.'s National Postsecondary Student Aid Study (NPSAS) is one such tool – a comprehensive, nationwide survey engineered to gather detailed data about student financial aid. The data extracted from NPSAS have unveiled the crushing weight of student debt on graduates, dictating their life choices – from postponing the purchase of homes to delaying the onset of family life.[17]

Longitudinal studies add another layer of depth to this understanding. The "Baccalaureate and Beyond" (B&B) study, conducted by the National Center for Education Statistics, tracks students for a decade after they earn their bachelor's degrees. This long-term observation provides invaluable insights into the ripple effects of student debt on their life trajectories, including career decisions, enrollment in graduate schools, and financial stability.[18]

Finally, economic models serve as a lens to scrutinize the interplay of market dynamics and tuition costs. As the hunger for higher education intensifies, economists have employed supply and demand models to understand its price implications. They've uncovered that as more jobs demand degrees, more individuals are willing to foot the bill for higher education – feeding the beast of rising costs. A 2021 report from the College Board[1] provided the latest trends in college pricing and student aid and showed that the average published tuition and fees for full-time undergraduate students increased by 1.6 percent at public four-year institutions, 1.5 percent at public four-year out-of-state institutions, and 1.3 percent at public two-year institutions in 2021–22. The report also showed that the average grant aid per full-time equivalent undergraduate student increased by 4.4 percent in 2020–21, while the average federal loan per borrower declined by 5.9 percent.

In sum, these various analytical tools and models provide a sophisticated understanding of the issue at hand. As the specter of rising higher education costs continues to loom large, these research strategies and innovative analytical approaches will play an increasingly vital role in paving the way toward effective solutions.

Looking Forward: A Rocky Road Ahead

The future of higher education costs casts a long shadow over students, universities, and governments alike. Over the years, the cost graph has been steadily ticking upward – a trajectory likely to persist in the years to come. With public funding for universities taking a nosedive in many nations, institutions are being cornered into seeking alternate revenue streams, sparking a surge in tuition fees and a heavier dependence on private capital.

The escalating costs of higher education present unique challenges that extend beyond the usual economic trends seen in other goods and services. This increase, especially pronounced due to the reduction in public funding, is forcing universities to explore alternative financial models. These models not only include raising tuition fees but also involve developing partnerships with private entities and expanding income-generating activities like research commercialization and international student recruitment. Such shifts are not just reshaping the financial landscape of higher education but also potentially altering the very nature of universities, raising questions about the balance between education as a public good and as a market-driven entity.

In the United States, reports from the College Board paint a grim picture: between 2008 and 2018, average tuition at public four-year colleges spiked by 37 percent.[19] Data from the European University Association echo similar trends, revealing significant slashes in public university funding in countries such as Italy and the UK.

The situation takes a bleaker turn as the global economy continues wrestling with the fallout of the COVID-19 pandemic. This crisis has stretched public finances to a breaking point and curtailed many families' ability to bear the brunt of skyrocketing higher education costs.

As a countermeasure, universities might redouble their efforts to woo international students, who typically bear heftier tuition fees, and tap into private funding.

However, these strategies are not without their pitfalls. A heavy reliance on international students leaves universities vulnerable to geopolitical tremors and changes in international student demographics. Meanwhile, the influx of private funding could stir up controversies around academic independence.

Given this, it's projected that universities will need to chart more diverse and resilient financial paths. They might find the way forward in expanding online offerings – potentially reaching more students at a fraction of the cost – forging stronger alliances with the private sector and alumni, and campaigning for heftier public investments in higher education.

Moreover, universities may ramp up efforts to fine-tune their financial aid systems, ensuring that academically promising students from disadvantaged backgrounds don't fall through the cracks. Such efforts could include rolling out more scholarships and introducing income-share agreements, a model where students pledge a portion of their future income to cover education costs. However, recent legislative and judicial actions in the United States have significantly impacted the landscape of affirmative action and diversity efforts in higher education.[20] This development has sparked debate and may potentially affect how universities design their financial aid and admission policies, particularly in their quest to promote diversity and equal opportunity in higher education.

In essence, while the ascending trajectory of higher education costs presents formidable hurdles, it also paves the way for unprecedented innovation and adaptability within universities. By doing so, these institutions can ensure that higher education remains within reach, continuing to fuel social mobility and economic progress in the face of adversity.

References

1 J. Ma and M. Pender, *Trends in College Pricing and Student Aid 2022* (New York: College Board, 2022).
2 S. Hubble and P. Bolton (2018). "Higher Education Tuition Fees in England," *Briefing Paper*, 8151, accessed May 19, 2024, https://researchbriefings.files.parliament.uk/documents/CBP-8151/CBP-8151.pdf.
3 "Overcoming Administrative Bloat in Higher Education," accessed August 14, 2023, https://academicinfluence.com/inflection/college-life/overcoming-administrative-bloat.
4 E. E. Cook and S. Turner (2023). "Progressivity of Pricing at US Public Universities," *Economics of Education Review*, 78, 102–116.
5 "State Higher Education Funding Cuts Have Pushed Costs to Students, Worsened Inequality," accessed August 14, 2023, https://www.cbpp.org/research/state-budget-and-tax/state-higher-education-funding-cuts-have-pushed-costs-to-students.
6 M. Hanson, "Student Loan Debt Statistics," *EducationData.org*, July 17, 2023, https://educationdata.org/student-loan-debt-statistics.
7 E. Burland, S. Dynarski, K. Michelmore, S. Owen, and S. Raghuraman (2023). "The Power of Certainty: Experimental Evidence on the Effective Design of Free Tuition Programs," *American Economic Review: Insights*, 5(3), 293–310.
8 "How Much Does It Cost to Study in Germany?" *Top Universities*, accessed December 30, https://www.topuniversities.com/student-info/student-finance/how-much-does-it-cost-study-germany.
9 M. Mitchell, M. Leachman, and K. Masterson (2017). "A Lost Decade in Higher Education Funding: State Cuts Have Driven Up Tuition and Reduced Quality",

Center on Budget and Policy Priorities, accessed June 17, 2024, https://www.cbpp.org/sites/default/files/atoms/files/2017_higher_ed_8-22-17_final.pdf

10 E. Gross (2020). "Administrative Bloat Meets the Coronavirus Pandemic," *American Council of Trustees and Alumni*, accessed May 19, 2024, https://www.goacta.org/2020/06/administrative-bloat-meets-the-coronavirus-pandemic/.

11 "Reimagining Higher Education in the United States," *Mckinsey & Company*, accessed December 16, 2023, https://www.mckinsey.com/industries/education/our-insights/reimagining-higher-education-in-the-united-states.

12 E. Rolen (2019). "Occupational Employment Projections through the Perspective of Education and Training," *The US Bureau of Labor Statistics*, January, accessed December 16, 2023, https://www.bls.gov/spotlight/2019/education-projections/home.htm.

13 S. Dynarski, C. J. Libassi, K. Michelmore, and S. Owen (2018). "Closing the Gap: The Effect of a Targeted, Tuition-Free Promise on College Choices of High-Achieving, Low-Income Students," *National Bureau of Economic Research*, No. w25349m, accessed December 16, 2023, https://www.nber.org/system/files/working_papers/w25349/w25349.pdf.

14 "Twenty to Life: As Federal Student Loan Interest Rate Hike Looms, New Research Shows Higher Education Turning into Multi-Decade Debt Sentence," *One Wisconsin Institute*, accessed December 16, 2023, https://onewisconsinnow.org/twenty-to-life-as-federal-student-loan-interest-rate-hike-looms-new-research-shows-higher-education-turning-into-multi-decade-debt-sentence/.

15 "IFS Finds Students Left with £50,800 Debt," accessed August 14, 2023, https://www.oxfordstudent.com/2017/07/09/ifs-finds-students-left-50800-debt/.

16 R. G. Ehrenberg (2012). "American Higher Education in Transition," *Journal of Economic Perspectives*, 26 (1): 193–216.

17 "National Postsecondary Student Aid Study - Overview," *U.S. Department of Education, Institute of Education Sciences*, accessed December 26, 2023, https://nces.ed.gov/surveys/npsas/.

18 "Baccalaureate and Beyond Longitudinal Study (B&B) - Overview," *National Center for Education Statistics*, accessed December 26, 2023, https://nces.ed.gov/surveys/b&b/.

19 M. Mitchell, M. Leachman, and M. Saenz (2019). "State Higher Education Funding Cuts Have Pushed Costs to Students, Worsened Inequality," *Center on Budget and Policy Priorities*, 24, 9–15.

20 "Advance Diversity and Opportunity in Higher Education: Justice and Education Departments Release Resources to Advance Diversity and Opportunity in Higher Education," *U.S. Department of Education*, accessed December 26, 2023, https://www.ed.gov/news/press-releases/advance-diversity-and-opportunity-higher-education-justice-and-education-departments-release-resources-advance-diversity-and-opportunity-higher-education.

5 The Age of Upheaval

Demographic Disruption: The Looming Storm and the Imperative for University Reinvention

The world stands at the precipice of an unprecedented demographic upheaval. As per the United Nations 2019 report, every eleventh person had crossed the age of sixty-five. This ratio is predicted to skyrocket to one in six by 2050.[1] Furthermore, World Bank data allude to a disquieting trend of falling fertility rates, particularly noticeable in East Asia and Europe.

For centuries, higher education has been the domain of late teens and early twenties. Now, a dwindling birth rate paints a dire portrait for universities. With fewer children in the pipeline, the reservoir of potential students shrinks, casting a long shadow over the future revenue and viability of these institutions.

Demographic changes are significantly impacting countries globally, with Japan exemplifying these challenges. The nation's youth population is declining due to low birth rates and an aging population. Data from the National Institute of Population and Social Security Research indicate that Japan's population aged fifteen to twenty-four is expected to decrease from around 15 million in 2015 to 7.9 million by 2060, a 47 percent reduction.[2] A 2023 report from *The Japan Times* highlighted concerns for universities, projecting that Japanese universities could see a fall by about 130,000 from 2022 in their enrollments between 2040 and 2050, which may affect their financial stability.[3]

Countries like South Korea and Thailand are in the same boat. Korea Higher Education Research Institute's research predicts a catastrophic 39 percent drop in South Korea's university-age population between 2020 and 2040.[4] The declining student numbers have already triggered a domino effect, with some universities being forced to slash admissions or shutter their doors entirely. Meanwhile, a study published in the *Journal of Population and Social Studies* foresees a sharp 25 percent decline in the number of new university students in Thailand from 2018 to 2032.[5]

DOI: 10.4324/9781003476504-6

In the face of a local demographic decline, Singapore has navigated a different course by reinventing itself as a global education hub. This small city-state, with a fertility rate of around 1.1 (the average number of children born per woman in a given population) in 2020, as per the Department of Statistics Singapore, has succeeded in offsetting the local demographic decline by attracting international students.[6]

In the UK, although there were fluctuations in birth rates in the early 2000s, according to data from the Office for National Statistics, the dip is set to rebound significantly in the subsequent decade.[7] The UK's active engagement in drawing international students might help cushion the impact of local demographic changes.

This demographic tumult, stoked by falling birth rates and aging populations, poses a grave challenge to the traditional model of university education worldwide. Universities must embrace this tide of change and adapt their offerings to cater to the new norm. Possible solutions could encompass an emphasis on lifelong learning, flexible learning models, and a concerted effort to draw in international students. Universities that neglect to act swiftly and adapt may soon find themselves grappling with budget constraints, forced closures, and a dwindling talent pool, ultimately impacting economies and industries at large.

Universities could pivot to face these challenges by tapping into strategies such as:

- Lifelong Learning: The World Economic Forum estimates that by 2022, a whopping 54 percent of all employees will need significant re- and up-skilling.[8] Universities could position themselves to cater to this demand by developing programs for older adults.
- Online Learning: The COVID-19 pandemic triggered an explosion in the growth of online learning platforms, expanding education's reach to a broader demographic.
- Collaboration with Industry: Strong ties with industry partners can help universities to ensure that the curriculum remains relevant and alluring to prospective students, thus fostering a new breed of students who are well prepared for the future job market.
- Research Focus: For some universities, the waning student populations may prompt them to focus more on research, thereby significantly contributing to the economy.

The changing demographics offer an opportunity for universities to transform their traditional models and evolve to meet the needs of a rapidly changing society. Failure to adapt could have far-reaching consequences, not just for the universities but also for the society at large. Yet, with challenge comes opportunity, and the shifting demographic landscape might just provide the catalyst for a new era of learning.

Silver Students: Navigating the Revolution of an Aging Learners Landscape

In a world grappling with the reality of an aging populace, universities sit on the precipice of a unique opportunity, one that has them looking at an older demographic in a way they've never had before. They've named this new breed of learners the "Silver Students." Data from the United Nations reveal a startling projection: the number of people aged sixty years or over, a figure that was at 1 billion in 2019, is projected to significantly increase to 1.4 billion by 2030.[1] It's an undeniable signal that the market for lifelong learning opportunities is about to explode.

The trend isn't just a local phenomenon; it's worldwide. A report that emerged from the National Center for Education Statistics in the United States laid it bare. Enrollment of students aged twenty-five and over in degree-granting postsecondary institutions ballooned by a whopping 35 percent between the years of 2000 and 2015.[9] Not to be outdone, the Organisation for Economic Co-operation and Development (OECD) fired a shot of its own in its "Education at a Glance" 2021 report, hammering home the point that lifelong learning has become an indispensable part of education systems, desperately trying to keep pace with a knowledge economy that seems to evolve faster than anyone can keep up with.[10]

Faced with this demographic sea change, universities are left with no choice but to adapt or get left behind. Certain institutions are being proactive. Harvard University accepted the challenge with its Institute for Learning in Retirement, while the University of Oxford followed suit with its Department for Continuing Education, both offering courses designed to cater to the personal enrichment, cultural interests, and professional development needs of these older adults.[11,12]

These silver students aren't just retirees looking for intellectual stimulation. They're career changers, ready to begin again in a new field. An American Institute for Economic Research study revealed that of the survey respondents aged forty-seven and older, a notable 82 percent successfully transitioned into new careers.[13] Institutions like the University of Minnesota were quick to seize the opportunity, launching its Advanced Careers (UMAC) initiative aimed squarely at preparing retirees for "encore careers" in community-focused roles.[14]

Beyond mere career advancement, the ripples of benefits that lifelong learning affords older adults are far-reaching. An intriguing study nestled within the pages of the *Research, Society and Development* uncovers that older adults who engage in lifelong-learning activities reap rewards such as improved cognitive function, bolstered mental well-being, and a surge in social activity. Universities that make the wise choice to offer a diverse range of personal enrichment courses could not only improve health outcomes and the quality of life for an aging population but also tap into an increasingly growing market.[15]

The evolution doesn't stop at the curriculum. Universities are facing a profound shift in teaching methods and course structures. They're becoming students of adult learning theories, such as Knowles' Andragogy, which emphasizes that adults learn most effectively when the education is self-directed and leverages their personal and professional experiences.[16] This approach ensures that their educational offerings are tailored to the unique learning styles of their older students, who benefit from autonomy and practical application in their learning process. Flexibility is the name of the game now, with universities exploring options like more flexible learning schedules, asynchronous learning, and credit for prior learning policies.

The dawn of the Silver Student era signals a tectonic shift for higher education institutions. By embracing this change, these institutions can harness a growing market, creating a vibrant ecosystem that nurtures lifelong learning and is attuned to the needs of an aging population. These aren't just minor adaptations; they're a reinvention of the system, one that could guarantee not just their survival but their relevance in this new world. In doing so, they're also helping shape the personal and professional growth of a demographic that's increasingly central to our societies.

Revamping the Ivory Tower: The Stakes and Strategies in the Fight for Future-Proofed Graduates

As we progress deeper into the Fourth Industrial Revolution, universities are facing the challenge of adapting to an era defined by rapid advancements in technology and significant economic shifts. They are tasked with ensuring that their academic programs remain relevant and rigorous, capable of preparing students for a job market that is continuously evolving due to technological innovations and economic changes. This situation requires universities to critically assess and update their curricula and teaching methods to meet the demands of the modern workforce.

The World Economic Forum's *Future of Jobs Report 2020*[8] offers a crucial perspective on the evolving job market. It underscores the imminent transformation in the labor landscape, driven by socioeconomic and technological changes. This shift signals a critical need for universities to adapt their curricula and approach, emphasizing skills that align with emerging job roles and industries. By focusing on reskilling and upskilling, universities can better prepare students for the dynamic future of work, where adaptability and continuous learning are key.

Adding to this narrative, the same WEF report maps out the skills that'll be worth their weight in gold come 2025: analytical thinking, innovation, complex problem solving, critical thinking, and analysis. Nipping at their heels will be self-management skills like active learning, resilience, stress tolerance, and flexibility.

McKinsey & Company's report, "The Future of Work after COVID-19," from 2021, offers similar findings. It projects a surge in demand for both rudimentary and advanced technological skills until 2030. All the while, social and emotional skills, the cornerstones of leadership and management, are predicted to see an uptick in demand.[17]

The task of shaping this brave new world falls heavily on universities' shoulders. They're no longer just information dispensaries; they're the guardians of the workforce of the future. Here's how they can live up to that monumental expectation.

- Joining Forces with Industry: Universities can't go it alone. By building strategic alliances with industries, they can calibrate their curriculum to the beat of the market's drum. The University of Cincinnati is a shining example, leading the pack with its cooperative education model. Their Division of Experience-Based Learning and Career Education brokers real-world work experiences such as internships, research projects, and social works, for students, enriching their academic journey and boosting their employability.[18]
- Getting Real with Experiential Learning: Merging real-world application and hands-on experiences into academic curricula is a masterstroke that can bridge the theory-practice divide. The University of Waterloo in Canada is a beacon in this regard, boasting one of the largest cooperative education programs globally that seamlessly marries academic and workplace learning.[19]
- Skills-Based Learning: Universities need to turn their focus to skills-based learning, ensuring graduates don't just have knowledge but employable competencies. MIT's "MicroMasters" programs embody this approach, honing industry-specific skills that can be applied on the job from day one.[20]
- Boosting Soft Skills: Universities can't afford to neglect soft skills like critical thinking, emotional intelligence, and leadership. Stanford University's Life Design Lab is a pioneer in this regard, introducing a unique curriculum that encourages the development of these essential skills.[21]
- Agility in Learning Models: In a job market that is rapidly and constantly evolving, universities must exhibit agility in their teaching models to stay relevant. This can range from short, intensive "bootcamp" style courses to online platforms for continuous skills upgrading, like Harvard University's HarvardX Initiative.[22]

As the workforce landscape changes and shifts, universities are being called to conduct a deep introspection and revamp of their traditional academic programs. By partnering with industry, focusing on experiential and skills-based learning, infusing soft skills, and adopting agile learning models, they can ensure their graduates not only land jobs but thrive in a transforming job market. The artful blending of these elements within academic programs will be crucial in nurturing a future workforce that is resilient, adaptable, and armed to tackle the challenges of the Fourth Industrial Revolution.

The Dance of Climate Change and Demographic Shifts

Higher education is standing on a precipice, staring into the face of two powerful global cyclones: climate change and demographic transitions. These titanic forces, formidable on their own, create additional challenges when they collide, pushing colleges and universities into unexplored wilds. No one can deny the physical, transition, and liability perils that climate change holds for higher education.

Natural disasters have had a considerable impact on higher education institutions, as exemplified by various incidents in recent years. For instance, the Camp fire in California in 2018 led to the closure of Butte College for more than two weeks, resulting in nearly $6.5 million in costs. This and other disasters such as hurricanes and floods have not only threatened lives and homes but also disrupted the educational journey of many students. These events have led to decreased enrollment and slowed progress toward graduation for students, and in some cases, financial strain for faculty and staff. Additionally, the response of educational institutions to these disasters has been crucial, often turning them into lifelines for affected students and the broader community. However, the recovery from such disasters can be a long-term process, spanning years or even decades.[23]

Universities in California, like the University of California, Berkeley, have faced significant challenges due to wildfires, such as the Northern California wildfires of 2017 and 2019. These events underscore the urgency for universities to incorporate climate change and environmental sustainability into their curricula. By doing so, they can prepare students to understand and address the causes and impacts of such natural disasters.[24] This approach not only enriches academic learning but also equips future leaders with the knowledge and skills necessary to tackle pressing global challenges like climate change.

Climate change isn't just triggering physical upheavals. It's also stirring up transitions. Consider Germany, where the government's pivot toward a low-carbon economy and the Energiewende (Energy Transition) have reshaped higher education.[25] Universities have had to revamp and launch new programs, focusing on renewable energy technologies, sustainable development, and environmental policy, to sync up with this change in national policy.

Lurking in the shadows are liability risks. In Australia, a twenty-four-year-old environmental scientist named Mark McVeigh made history by suing his pension fund for failing to disclose or assess climate change's impact on its investments.[26] This legal action shines a spotlight on the potential legal landmines institutions could trigger if they turn a blind eye to climate mitigation or adaptation.

Reputational risks are another frontier. A 2020 report by People & Planet blew the lid off the fact that UK universities have £12.4 billion tied up in fossil fuel and high-carbon industries.[27] Such investments risk tarnishing their image and deterring environmentally minded students and staff.

In essence, climate change is a many-headed beast for higher education, bringing physical damage from climate disasters, transition requirements, and potential legal and reputational risks. Universities need to acknowledge these threats and plot a proactive course to mitigate their risk and secure their future sustainability.

On the flip side, demographic transitions pose their own set of daunting challenges for higher education, mainly through their grip on student enrollment numbers. The fallout from declining birth rates on university enrollments is a reality in many countries.

Take the United States, where a report by the Western Interstate Commission for Higher Education flagged a downturn in high school graduates from 2020 onward, with the trend expected to persist till at least 2032. These demographic waves directly impact the pool of potential university entrants, with certain states in the Midwest and Northeast projected to witness a jaw-dropping 25 percent decline in high school graduates by 2032. The decline in the number of high school graduates in the United States, as projected by the Western Interstate Commission for Higher Education, is attributed mainly to a decrease in birth rates. Since the Great Recession, there has been a consistent 1 percent yearly decrease in births, leading to a predicted reduction in high school graduates. By the class of 2037, it's expected that there will be 11 percent fewer graduates compared to previous years. This trend is not uniform across the country; regions like the Midwest and Northeast are expected to see more significant declines, while the South and West may experience varied patterns of change. Additionally, the changing demographics of high school graduates, with increases in non-white graduates, will affect college enrollment strategies, particularly in community colleges, and transfer student recruitment.[28]

Japan presents another cautionary tale. The country's Ministry of Education, Culture, Sports, Science and Technology projected a significant 52 percent dip in the eighteen-year-old population from 1992 to 2022.[29] This decline, primarily spurred by dwindling fertility rates, has monumental implications for Japanese higher education, sparking fierce competition for students and posing grave sustainability challenges, especially for universities in rural areas.

Europe isn't spared either. Eurostat data reveal a drop in the young population (fifteen to twenty-four years old) in the EU from 64 million in 2005 to 56 million in 2020.[30] The shrinkage of this group, the lifeblood of university undergraduate entrants, calls for a serious rethink of higher education.

However, the shifting demographics also present a silver lining, opening up opportunities for universities to cater to mature learners and international students. The rising global middle class, particularly in Asia, has led to a surge in the number of international students flocking to Western universities. OECD data confirm this trend, showing that the number of international students worldwide jumped from 2.6 million in 2000 to 4.4 million in 2021, with the uptrend expected to hold course.[31]

Universities are facing a complex challenge as they navigate the impacts of climate change and demographic shifts. They must adapt to a student population that is both shrinking and aging, while simultaneously addressing and integrating the realities of climate change into their curricula and campus operations. This situation requires a delicate balance between meeting the educational needs of a diverse student body and responding proactively to environmental concerns.

With these challenges, a curious pattern emerges – universities have the opportunity to call the shots on the subject of climate change mitigation and adaptation. An example of such leadership is Columbia University, with its avant-garde Climate School established in 2020.[32] This forward-thinking move targets climate issues through a multidisciplinary approach, combining education, research, and public-private partnerships. The school is bent on fueling the shift to sustainability and resilience, molding a new legion of leaders equipped to crack the climate crisis code.

Furthermore, an aging demographic presents an unsung market for higher education. With the demographic scales tipping, universities can concoct lifelong learning programs tailor-made for older adults, with an emphasis on climate change education. A model worth examining is Stanford University's Distinguished Careers Institute. The program invites seasoned leaders for a yearlong sojourn at Stanford to reflect and study, offering courses with a social impact spin, often featuring climate change education.[33]

Universities can also play a pivotal role in steering societal adaptation to climate change. This becomes all the more critical given the heightened vulnerability of older populations to extreme weather events. For instance, the University of South Florida's College of Public Health is honing research related to climate change's impact on public health, including heat-related illnesses, and disseminating these findings to the broader community.[34]

Moreover, universities can tap into their outreach prowess and forge collaborative ventures to aid communities in beefing up their resilience to climate-related threats. One such beacon of effort is the University of Arizona's Agnese Nelms Haury Program in Environment and Social Justice. The initiative bolsters partnerships between the university and community organizations to tackle the challenges sprung by environmental shifts.[35]

The tangle of climate change and demographic shifts can indeed pitch significant hurdles at higher education institutions. However, within these challenges lies the seed for transformative change. Universities can harness their distinctive position to steer climate change mitigation and adaptation initiatives while also catering to evolving student demographics. With strategic maneuvers, a commitment to sustainability, and engaging with communities, universities can carve a path through these twin challenges.

Predictions and Prognosis

If one stares long enough at the data, trends, and the searing reality of the numbers, it becomes evident that the trending demographic will deal a punishing blow to the world of higher education. Universities, especially in nations like Japan, South Korea, and Thailand, are hurtling toward an enrollment famine. The dwindling youth population threatens the very lifeblood of these institutions. Small universities, in particular, stand at the precipice, with survival at stake.

But as they say, every crisis seeds an opportunity. The sweeping tide of an aging society presents a ripe chance for lifelong learning initiatives to take root. It will no longer be about late teens and early twenties. Academia must brace itself to cater to adults juggling work commitments and retirees looking to satiate their thirst for knowledge. We might witness the likes of the University of the Third Age, where older adults flock to learn and multiply across the globe.

Another lifebuoy thrown at the universities in these turbulent times comes in the form of online learning. The onslaught of COVID-19 saw the rise of virtual classrooms. The quiet, steady humming of servers replaced the cacophony of buzzing campuses. Universities will need to seize this digital dawn to reach far and wide, well beyond the confines of their brick-and-mortar classrooms. Investments will need to be pumped into technological infrastructure and pedagogical strategies to provide an enriching and effective online learning experience.

Online learning, accelerated by the pandemic, is not just a temporary fix but a long-term expansion of higher education's reach. The transition to virtual classrooms has highlighted the potential for universities to access a broader, more diverse student base, including nontraditional learners and international students. Going forward, the challenge for universities lies not just in technological investments but in creatively integrating online and traditional learning methods to provide a more inclusive, flexible, and personalized educational experience.

Bridging the gap between the world of academia and industry will take on an urgency like never before. Universities, if they hope to keep their coffers from running dry, must align themselves with industry trends. Close collaboration with industries, work-integrated learning experiences, relevant curriculum, and robust career services must form the backbone of the academic experience.

With the local student well running dry, the need for survival might push universities to cast their net wider and search for international students. Cultivating an inclusive environment and fostering cross-cultural exchange would be essential to lure students across the borders. Equally important would be fostering international collaborations, to bolster reputation and rankings.

Perhaps the greatest pivot might come in the form of universities shifting their focus to research and innovation. They may need to shun the traditional student-dependent model and instead position themselves as centers of technological advancements and scientific breakthroughs. Policymakers and funding agencies will need to recognize the importance of research investment.

Last, but certainly not least, will be the pressing need for universities to reinvent their financial models. The threat of dried-up enrollment and skyrocketing costs might compel them to think outside the box. Professional development programs, consulting services, and licensing of intellectual property could emerge as significant revenue streams. Endowments and philanthropy will have a critical role to play, underpinning the financial stability of higher education.

Universities are at a critical juncture, grappling with the fallout of changing demographics. Their survival will hinge on their ability to adapt to lifelong learning, embrace online education, foster industry collaboration, attract international students, and accentuate research. Demographic change could lead to financial instability, curtailed access to quality education, and diminished competitiveness, dealing a crippling blow to societal progress. Therefore, it becomes incumbent upon universities, governments, and stakeholders to join forces and pave the way for innovation, inclusivity, and lifelong learning to ensure a robust future for higher education.

References

1 United Nations (2019). "Ageing," *United Nations*, accessed May 19, 2024, https://www.un.org/en/global-issues/ageing.
2 National Institute of Population and Social Security Research in Japan (2012). "Population Projections for Japan (January 2012), 2011 to 2060," accessed May 19, 2024, https://www.ipss.go.jp/site-ad/index_english/esuikei/ppfj2012.pdf.
3 "Japan University Admissions Seen Falling by 130,000 by 2040s," *The Japan Times*, accessed December 16, 2023, https://www.japantimes.co.jp/news/2023/07/15/national/university-student-decline-survey/.
4 "As Student Numbers Drop, Experts Mull University Closures," accessed August 14, 2023, https://www.universityworldnews.com/post.php?story=20230526142304142.
5 "Thailand's Low Birthrate Is Affecting Enrolments at Thai Universities," accessed August 14, 2023, https://www.nationthailand.com/thailand/general/40028813.
6 "Births And Fertility Rates," accessed by August 14, 2023, https://tablebuilder.singstat.gov.sg/table/TS/M810091.
7 "Annual Birth Rates from 2000 to 2016," *Office for National Statistics*, accessed December 16, 2023, https://www.ons.gov.uk/aboutus/transparencyandgovernance/freedomofinformationfoi/annualbirthratesfrom2000to2016.

8 "The Future of Jobs Report 2020," accessed July 30, 2023, https://weforum.org/reports/the-future-of-jobs-report-2020/.
9 "Total Fall Enrollment in Degree-Granting Postsecondary Institutions, by Attendance Status, Sex, And Age of Student: Selected Years, 2001 Through 2031," accessed August 14, 2023, https://nces.ed.gov/programs/digest/d22/tables/dt22_303.40.asp.
10 "Education at a Glance 2021: OECD Indicators.", OECD iLibrary, accessed December 26, 2023, https://www.oecd-ilibrary.org/education/education-at-a-glance-2021_f05ff492-en.
11 "Harvard Division of Continuing Education," *Harvard Institute for Learning in Retirement*, accessed December 30, https://hilr.dce.harvard.edu/.
12 "University of Oxford Department for Continuing Education," accessed December 30, https://www.conted.ox.ac.uk/.
13 American Institute for Economic Research (2015). "New Careers for Older Workers," accessed May 19, 2024, https://www.aier.org/wp-content/uploads/2015/09/newcareersolderworkers-aier.pdf.
14 "University of Minnesota Advanced Careers (UMAC)." *University of Minnesota*, accessed December 26, 2023, https://umac.umn.edu/.
15 K. L. Flauzino, H. M. P. T. Gil, S. S. T. Batistoni, M. O. Costa, and M. Cachioni (2021). "Lifelong Learning Activities for Older Adults: A Scoping Review Protocol," *Research, Society and Development*, 10(14), e2194721947.
16 A. El-Amin (2020). "Andragogy: A Theory in Practice in Higher Education," *Journal of Research in Higher Education*, 4(2), 54–69.
17 "The Future of Work after COVID-19," *Mckinsey & Company*, accessed December 16, 2023, https://www.mckinsey.com/featured-insights/future-of-work/the-future-of-work-after-covid-19.
18 "Co-op at the University of Cincinnati," *University of Cincinnati*, accessed December 26, 2023. https://www.uc.edu/co-op.html.
19 "Co-operative Education," *University of Waterloo*, accessed December 26, 2023, https://uwaterloo.ca/co-operative-education/.
20 "MITx MicroMasters Programs," *Massachusetts Institute of Technology*, accessed December 26, 2023, https://micromasters.mit.edu/.
21 "Stanford Life Design Lab," *Stanford Life Design Lab*, accessed December 26, 2023, https://lifedesignlab.stanford.edu/.
22 "HarvardX," *Harvard Initiative for Learning and Teaching*, accessed December 26, 2023, https://hilt.harvard.edu/teaching-learning-resources/harvard-x/.
23 "What Has Happened When Campuses Shut Down for Other Disasters? A Coronavirus Case Study," *The Hechinger Report*, accessed December 16, 2023, https://hechingerreport.org/what-has-happened-when-campuses-shut-down-for-other-disasters-a-coronavirus-case-study/.
24 "As Wildfires Worsen, Berkeley Students and Alumni Team Up with First Responders to Solve Information Challenges," *Blum Center for Developing Economies, University of California, Berkeley*, accessed December 26, 2023, https://blumcenter.berkeley.edu/students-alum-solve-wildfire-challenges/.
25 "The Social Impact of Germany's Energy Transition," *Clean Energy Wire*, accessed December 26, 2023, https://www.cleanenergywire.org/dossiers/social-impact-germanys-energy-transition.
26 "Rest Reaches Settlement with Mark McVeigh." *Rest Super*, accessed December 26, 2023, https://rest.com.au/why-rest/about-rest/news/rest-reaches-settlement-with-mark-mcveigh.
27 "British Universities to Divest from Fossil Fuels," accessed August 14, 2023, https://global.chinadaily.com.cn/a/202001/14/WS5e1d2a59a310128217270c15.html.

28 "Knocking at the College Door—Projections of High School Graduates through 2037," *Western Interstate Commission for Higher Education*, accessed December 16, 2023, https://www.wiche.edu/resources/a-knocking-update-covid-19-and-public-school-enrollments-and-graduates/.
29 "MEXT Releases the Results of the FY2022 School Basic Survey," accessed August 14, 2023, https://www.nicjp.niad.ac.jp/en/news/schoolbasicsurvey2022.html.
30 "Youth Population on 1 January by Sex, Age and Country of Birth," accessed August 14, 2023, https://ec.europa.eu/eurostat/web/products-datasets/-/yth_demo_060.
31 "Rising International Student Mobility," accessed August 14, 2023, https://www.oecd.org/coronavirus/en/data-insights/rising-international-student-mobility.
32 "Columbia to Establish a Climate School to Meet the Challenges of a Warming World." *State of the Planet, Columbia University Earth Institute*, accessed December 26, 2023, https://news.climate.columbia.edu/2020/07/10/columbia-establish-climate-school-meet-challenges-warming-world/.
33 "Home - Stanford Distinguished Careers Institute," *Stanford DCI*, accessed December 26, 2023, https://dci.stanford.edu/.
34 "Research," USF Health, *College of Public Health*, accessed December 26, 2023, https://health.usf.edu/publichealth/activist-lab.
35 "Home - Agnese Nelms Haury Program in Environment and Social Justice," accessed December 26, 2023, https://www.haury.arizona.edu/.

6 When AI Stakes Its Claim in Higher Education

Reimagining Teaching with AI

The world of education is under a transformative siege, an AI-driven revolution fueled by the thirst for personalization, the challenge of scale, and the pursuit of excellence. And it's a revolution that doesn't exist in isolation – it is a reflection of a society swept by the digital tide, with educational institutions hustling to keep up. While AI-driven educational tools are revolutionizing personalized learning, critics argue that they can also depersonalize experiences. There is a growing debate about the balance between using AI to tailor educational content to individual needs and maintaining the human element that fosters deeper understanding and empathy. It's crucial for educational institutions to navigate this dichotomy, ensuring that while they leverage AI for efficiency and scale, they also preserve the essential human interactions that form the core of the educational experience.

The "Artificial Intelligence Market in the North America Education Sector 2022–27" report reveals an astounding surge of 43 percent in the AI education market.[1] This shift can be attributed largely to the adoption of cloud-based AI solutions, painting a clear picture of the growing hunger for AI-powered teaching methods.

Welcome to the age of adaptive learning platforms like MATHia, Knewton, and DreamBox Learning.[2–4] Tailored learning experiences are the name of the game. The MATHia software, designed by Carnegie Learning, has been recognized for significantly boosting Algebra I End-of-Course performance. Specifically, the median student experienced a 16 percentile point improvement, effectively moving from the 50th to the 66th percentile, showcasing the substantial academic benefits offered by this AI-driven tutoring software.[5] The secret machine-learning algorithms that handcraft problems for individual students, match their pace, and deliver real-time feedback.

When it comes to grading, AI has been nothing short of a revolution, taking the reins of efficiency, fairness, and objectivity. Take Gradescope, a pioneering venture by Turnitin. As per a 2017 report by UC Berkeley, the introduction of Gradescope saw grading time cut by 30 percent, boosting instructional efficiency.[6]

DOI: 10.4324/9781003476504-7

The stage is also set for AI-driven essay-grading tools. The likes of Project Essay Grade (PEG) and ETS's e-rater are gaining traction. The latter garnered attention when it reportedly concurred with human graders 97 percent of the time, as per a 2022 study in the *Journal of Technology, Learning, and Assessment*.[7]

But what set the wheels of this AI revolution in motion? The COVID-19 pandemic played a critical role. Education was thrust online, underlining the need for tools that could scale, personalize learning, and grade efficiently. The pandemic opened the floodgates for AI integration in education.

Further fueling the AI revolution has been the growing investments in EdTech startups and an increase in AI tool availability. EdX and Coursera – the two towering titans in the world of Massive Open Online Courses (MOOCs) – marked a significant milestone in 2022. They embraced AI tools extensively in their course delivery, signaling a sea change in higher education's approach.[8,9]

Teaching in higher education has been swept by an AI-driven transformation. A perfect storm of societal digitization, shifts in educational delivery borne by the pandemic, a wave of investment in EdTech, and the undeniably effective AI tools have set the stage for a revolution. Buckle up, because this ride is just beginning.

The Professor Reinvented: AI's Impact on Academia

Higher education, riding the wave of AI's advancements, is witnessing a metamorphosis in the role of its professors. But contrary to popular imagination, AI isn't stepping into professors' shoes – it's giving them a new, potent set of tools and expanding their sphere of influence.

A 2021 study by the *International Journal of Educational Technology in Higher Education* threw a startling statistic into the spotlight: Educators are exploring ways to effectively integrate AI tools into their teaching practices, balancing the benefits of AI with the need to maintain academic integrity and the quality of education.[10]

Jill Watson, the AI teaching assistant at Georgia Tech, is primarily used for answering students' frequently asked questions and handling a large volume of routine queries that would otherwise take up a significant amount of a professor's time. By swiftly and accurately responding to these questions, Jill Watson reduces the administrative burden on professors. This efficiency allows faculty members to focus more on in-depth mentorship, engage in meaningful discussions, and foster critical thinking skills among students. The impact of this AI tool is reflected in student feedback, where 80 percent have noticed an improvement in professor mentorship and engagement levels due to the reduced administrative load on faculty.[11]

But AI's revolution isn't confined to the classroom – it's an indispensable ally in the realm of research. A 2023 *Science* report unveiled that researchers using AI experienced a productivity boost of a notable 40 percent.[12] Look at the complex systems prediction by MIT researchers, supercharged by Google's DeepMind AI model, that is reshaping fields as diverse as quantum physics and molecular biology. Or consider the avalanche of data in social sciences that AI has deciphered, unearthing insights into socioeconomic disparities and the intricate dance of human behavior.

Universities aren't just leveraging AI – they're nurturing it. Case in point: the University of Michigan's AI labs. Here, students and professors roll up their sleeves, collaborating on AI projects, experimenting, and innovating. These labs are the hothouses of hands-on learning, fostering a deeper comprehension of AI's real-world applications.[13]

Despite the rapid advancement of AI, it still does not surpass the capabilities of a human professor in many aspects of teaching and academic mentorship. Professors bring to the table mentorship, the ability to ignite creativity, and emotional support, qualities that AI can't replicate.

Beyond academics, professors are the architects of a sense of community, inclusivity, and belongingness among students. A 2022 study by the *Journal of Higher Education* underscored this, revealing that students with strong faculty relationships were 1.9 times more likely to persevere in their studies.[14]

Certain watershed events have accelerated AI's march into academia, most notably the COVID-19 pandemic. The sudden transition to online learning spotlighted AI's potential in taking over mundane tasks, empowering professors to shift focus to mentorship and personalized guidance.

Coupled with growing investments and strides in AI research, the AI wave has shown no signs of abating. AI labs are sprouting up in universities, like at the University of Michigan, a testament to the recognition of AI's significance in education and research.

In summary, while AI is making impressive strides in higher education, it's not out to replace professors. Rather, it's enhancing their roles, underlining the irreplaceability of the human touch in teaching, mentorship, and learning. Professors find themselves at a thrilling crossroads, their roles expanding in unforeseen ways, necessitating adaptability, and igniting the same in their students. And so, the age-old profession of the professor is being reinvented, with AI as the catalyst.

Behind the Scenes: AI's Makeover of University Administration

Artificial intelligence is painting a new picture of university operations – efficient, personalized, and smart. Universities aren't just about education anymore. They're rapidly evolving into "smart institutions," with AI-powered systems at the helm of administration.

To comprehend the significance of AI in university operations, consider this. According to the National Center for Education Statistics, between 2000 and 2017, enrollment in degree-granting postsecondary institutions increased by a substantial 23 percent.[15] As the student population burgeons, the need for efficient, streamlined administration has never been more critical – and AI is stepping in to fill that role.

EDUCAUSE's 2022 report presented a revealing statistic: 47 percent of higher education institutions in the United States were harnessing AI to amplify their student services. And the trend isn't slowing down – another 42 percent plan to join the bandwagon within the next three years.[16]

Take Georgia State University's AI chatbot, Pounce, for instance. This AI-powered marvel was a game-changer in reducing "summer melt" rates by 22 percent in 2016.[17] Pounce isn't just a chatbot; it's a virtual assistant that guides students, reminds them of crucial deadlines, and provides personalized advice.

But AI's administrative wonders aren't limited to student services. The enrollment and financial aid processes are also undergoing an AI revolution. With intelligent automation, application reviews and aid distributions are faster and more accurate, freeing up administrative staff for other tasks. The University of Arizona, for instance, relies on AI to speed up the financial aid process, delivering faster and more precise financial aid packages to students.

AI's prowess extends to optimizing resource allocation and scheduling. The AI-based scheduling platform by Ad Astra is a case in point. Juggling variables like faculty availability, class size, and classroom capacity optimizes resource use. A McKinsey report from 2022 confirms that institutions leveraging AI for scheduling have witnessed efficiency gains of 33 percent.[18]

The University of South Florida's predictive analytics system, SAM, represents another innovative AI application – predicting student outcomes. Analyzing over 800 variables to predict student success equips administrators to provide proactive support where needed most.[19]

Despite its many victories, AI isn't without its Achilles heel. Data privacy and the ethical use of AI stand out as major challenges. The 2023 paper in the *Journal of Higher Education Policy and Management*[20] emphasizes the critical need for comprehensive policies in universities regarding AI use. It advocates for frameworks that not only focus on the ethical deployment of AI in educational settings but also prioritize the protection of students' and staff members' data. The paper highlights the growing integration of AI in university teaching and learning and addresses the complexities this brings in terms of ethics and data security. It calls for a balanced approach that leverages the benefits of AI while managing its risks and ensuring ethical standards are upheld in the academic environment.

Moreover, a dark cloud looms on the horizon – the digital divide. UNESCO's 2023 report highlights that students from lower-income countries, where AI tools aren't as readily available, may find themselves in the academic shadows of their counterparts from developed nations.[21]

Furthermore, a 2022 Educause report reveals that 75 percent of universities see student data privacy as a growing problem.[15] The ethical minefield around AI includes issues like algorithmic bias, transparency, and the potential impact on academia's employment landscape.

AI's presence in university administration is spreading rapidly, promising greater efficiency, personalized services, and an enhanced student experience. As institutions grapple with the ethical and implementation challenges that come with AI, its role in higher education is set to become increasingly significant. However, as with all technological advances, a careful balance needs to be struck between innovation and privacy, access, and ethics.

A Glimpse into the Future: AI's Ascendancy in Higher Education

The significant growth in the AI in education market, as reported by MarketsandMarkets, highlights a major shift in higher education. This projected increase from $1.82 billion in 2021 to $3.68 billion by 2023 indicates a strong commitment from educational institutions to integrate AI.[22] This integration is not just for operational efficiency or research enhancement; it's increasingly seen as key to enriching the learning experience. The investment reflects the belief in AI's potential to transform various aspects of education, signaling a major evolution in how teaching and learning are approached in the modern educational landscape.

Several universities have already ventured into this uncharted territory. Sacramento State University is pioneering in the field of AI in education with the launch of the National Institute for Artificial Intelligence in Education (I-AI). This institute, led by Dr. Alexander Sidorkin, aims to advance the use and ethical application of AI in educational settings. It focuses on integrating AI into teaching, learning, advising, and student support services. The institute aims to utilize AI's power for training students in its ethical application, reimagining coursework to enhance the success of underserved students, and establishing programs to share resources and ethical guidelines on AI with educators in K–12 and higher education. This initiative reflects Sacramento State's commitment to being at the forefront of incorporating AI into education, ensuring their students and faculty are equipped to handle the challenges and opportunities presented by AI technology.[23] At Carnegie Mellon University, the AI tutor "Alex" utilizes machine learning to offer a personalized feedback system. Alex adapts to individual student needs, providing customized assistance and improving educational outcomes.[24] These AI applications represent advancements in educational technology, offering innovative, responsive, and personalized learning experiences.

Artificial intelligence is significantly transforming the landscape of research and administrative tasks in universities. For example, Stanford University employs AI to process large datasets in diverse research fields like climate change, genetics, and neuroscience.[25,26] This use of AI enables more efficient analysis and deeper insights, drastically altering traditional research methodologies. AI's impact could also extend beyond research, enhancing various operational aspects of university administration, streamlining processes, and improving efficiency.[27]

Yet, as AI integrates itself into higher education, it's imperative to remember that it's a double-edged sword. In a 2020 survey by the Online Learning Consortium, a resounding 68 percent of educators were of the view that the deployment of AI in education should be regulated by an ethical code.[28] The issues on the table range from privacy worries and the risk of algorithmic bias, to the unshakeable need for human oversight.

Equity also remains a significant concern. The advent of AI could inadvertently widen the digital divide. A report from EDUCAUSE in 2019 raises the specter of education equity, highlighting that not all students can access the necessary technology to reap the benefits of AI-powered learning.[29]

However, with a strategic and considered adoption, AI could bring about a revolution in higher education. Personalized learning, once a lofty ideal, could become the new normal. Picture an AI system that assesses a student's interaction with an online platform, tweaking the learning experience to fit their unique needs. This level of customization could ramp up engagement and improve learning outcomes dramatically.

As we consider the future of AI in higher education, one thing is clear: the human element remains indispensable. As pointed out by a Deloitte Insights report, "skills that are uniquely human—creativity, leadership, empathy—are difficult to automate and are likely to become more valuable as AI and automation become more prevalent."[30]

In conclusion, AI's role in higher education's future is immense and promising, provided its integration is handled with an eye for ethics and inclusivity. As the wheels of this technological revolution keep turning, higher education stands on the precipice of a transformative leap. And while we're on this journey, let's not forget – technology should serve us, not the other way around.

References

1 "Artificial Intelligence (AI) Market in the Education Sector by End-User, Learning Method and Geography-Forecast and Analysis 2023–27," accessed August 14, 2023, https://www.technavio.com/report/artificial-intelligence-market-in-the-education-sector-industry-analysis.
2 "Knewton Is Building the World's Smartest Tutor," accessed September 5, 2023, https://www.forbes.com/sites/bruceupbin/2012/02/22/knewton-is-building-the-worlds-smartest-tutor/?sh=26df157717a7.

3 "DreamBox Learning Achievement Growth in the Howard County Public School System and Rocketship Education" (2016), *Center for Education Policy at Harvard University*, accessed September 5, 2023, https://cepr.harvard.edu/publications/dreambox-learning-achievement-growth.
4 Carnegie Learning (2021). "MATHia," accessed December 16, 2023, https://www.carnegielearning.com/solutions/math/mathia/
5 "Carnegie Learning Announces New 3rd Party Study Indicating That MATHia Leads to Better Performance in Algebra" (2021), *Business Wire*, accessed May 19, 2024, https://www.businesswire.com/news/home/20210721005130/en/Carnegie-Learning-Announces-New-3rd-Party-Study-Indicating-That-MATHia-Leads-to-Better-Performance-in-Algebra.
6 A. Singh, S. Karayev, K. Gutowski, and P. Abbeel (April 2017). "Gradescope: A Fast, Flexible, and Fair System for Scalable Assessment of Handwritten Work," In *Proceedings of the Fourth (2017) ACM Conference on Learning @ Scale, Cambridge Massachusetts USA* (pp. 81–88).
7 J. Chen, M. Zhang, and I. I. Bejar (2017). "An Investigation of the e-rater® Automated Scoring Engine's Grammar, Usage, Mechanics, and Style Microfeatures and Their Aggregation Model," *ETS Research Report Series*, 2017(1), 1–14.
8 "edX Impact Report," accessed December 26, 2023, https://impact.edx.org/2022.
9 "Coursera: Online Courses From Top Universities," accessed December 26, 2023, https://www.coursera.org/.
10 K. Seo, J. Tang, I. Roll, S. Fels, and D. Yoon (2021). "The Impact of Artificial Intelligence on Learner–Instructor Interaction in Online Learning," *International Journal of Educational Technology in Higher Education*, 18(1), 1–23.
11 "One of the TAs in an Artificial Intelligence Class Was Actually an A.I.," accessed August 14, 2023, https://slate.com/technology/2016/05/a-teaching-assistant-at-georgia-tech-was-actually-an-artificial-intelligence.html.
12 S. Noy and W. Zhang (2023). "Experimental Evidence on the Productivity Effects of Generative Artificial Intelligence," *Science*, 381(6654), 187–192.
13 "Michigan AI Laboratory," accessed December 16, 2023, https://ai.engin.umich.edu/.
14 R. Tormey (2021). "Rethinking Student-Teacher Relationships in Higher Education: A Multidimensional Approach," *Higher Education*, 82(4), 993–1011.
15 "Total Undergraduate Fall Enrollment in Degree-Granting Postsecondary Institutions, by Attendance Status, Sex of Student, and Control and Level of Institution: Selected Years, 1970 through 2030," accessed August 14, 2023, https://nces.ed.gov/programs/digest/d21/tables/dt21_303.70.asp.
16 K. Pelletier, M. McCormack, J. Reeves, J. Robert, N. Arbino, C. Dickson-Deane, and J. Stine (2022). "2022 EDUCAUSE Horizon Report Teaching and Learning Edition" (pp. 1–58), accessed August 14, 2023, https://pdfs.semanticscholar.org/b6cc/95802cdd4bbb2f16290b58f0e936aa019104.pdf.
17 "Reduction of Summer Melt," accessed August 14, 2023, https://success.gsu.edu/initiatives/reduction-of-summer-melt/.
18 "Smart Scheduling: How to Solve Workforce-Planning Challenges with AI," accessed August 14, 2023, https://www.mckinsey.com/capabilities/operations/our-insights/smart-scheduling-how-to-solve-workforce-planning-challenges-with-ai.
19 "System for Assessment Management (SAM), University of South California," accessed December 16, 2023, https://usfweb.usf.edu/DSS/SAM/.
20 "Micro-Credential Approval, Accreditation and Listing," *New Zealand Qualifications Authority*, accessed December 16, 2023, https://www2.nzqa.govt.nz/tertiary/approval-accreditation-and-registration/micro-credentials/.
21 "Global Education Monitoring Report Summary, 2023," accessed December 26, https://www.unesdoc.unesco.org/ark:/48223/pf0000386147.

22 "AI in Education Market Report," accessed August 14, 2023, https://www.marketsandmarkets.com/Market-Reports/ai-in-education-market-200371366.html.
23 "Sac State President Wood Announces Formation of New Artificial Intelligence Institute and Its 'czar' as University Moves to Take Lead in AI Education," accessed December 16, 2023, https://www.csus.edu/news/newsroom/stories/2023/12/ai-in-education.html.
24 "New AI Enables Teachers to Rapidly Develop Intelligent Tutoring Systems," *Carnegie Mellon University News*, accessed December 16, 2023, https://www.cmu.edu/news/stories/archives/2020/april/ai-teaching.html.
25 "Stanford Woods Institute for the Environment," accessed December 30, https://woods.stanford.edu/.
26 "Wu Tsai Neurosciences Institute at Stanford University (n.d.)," *Wu Tsai Neurosciences Institute*, accessed December 30, https://neuroscience.stanford.edu/.
27 P. Parycek, V. Schmid, and A. S. Novak (2023). "Artificial Intelligence (AI) and Automation in Administrative Procedures: Potentials, Limitations, and Framework Conditions," *Journal of the Knowledge Economy*. https://doi.org/10.1007/s13132-023-01433-3
28 Australian Human Rights Commission (2023). "Utilising Ethical AI in the Australian Education System," accessed December 16, 2023, https://humanrights.gov.au/sites/default/files/inquiry_into_the_use_of_generative_artificial_intelligence_in_the_australian_education_system_14_july_2023_0.pdf.
29 B. Alexander, K. A.-Rowe, N. B.-Murphy, G. Dobbin, J. K. M. McCormack, J. Pomerantz, R. Seilhamer, and N. Weber (2019). "EDUCAUSE horizon report: 2019 higher education edition." Louisville, CO: EDUCAUSE. https://library.educause.edu/resources/2019/4/2019-horizon-report
30 "Deloitte Insights: AI, Robotics, and Intelligent Machines," accessed December 16, 2023, https://www2.deloitte.com/us/en/insights/focus/human-capital-trends/2018/ai-robotics-intelligent-machines.html.

7 Balancing the Scale
AI-Led Education's Promise and Perils

The AI Equation: Promises Made, Promises Kept, and Shadows Cast

The effectiveness of AI in education, as demonstrated by platforms like Knewton, shows promising results. In 2012, Knewton's technology helped increase college students' pass rates from 66 percent to 75 percent, while reducing dropout rates from 13 percent to 6 percent.[1] This notable improvement was reinforced by a 2019 survey where 77 percent of teachers acknowledged that digital technology significantly enhances student engagement.[2] These developments indicate the impactful role of AI and digital tools in transforming educational outcomes.

Meanwhile, on the other side of the globe, China was watching and learning. A 2018 policy edict, the "AI Development Plan," steered the country toward the integration of AI into public services. This policy maneuver made room for Squirrel AI's ascent. By 2020, this adaptive learning platform, with its personalized learning plan, had catapulted student mathematics test scores upward by 15 percent.[3]

The case for AI-led education finds further credence in the learning efficiency it brings to the table. A 2015 study by the Gates Foundation found that students using adaptive learning technologies have made significant gains in mathematics and reading, outpacing their traditionally taught peers by 11 percent and 8 percent, respectively.[4]

Fast forward to 2022, and we find Coursera boasting a worldwide user base of 118 million,[5] edX competing keenly, and in India, Byju's reaching for the stars with a remarkable 70 million users.[6] These platforms are leveraging the gig economy's rise and the ensuing need for continual skill updating to cement AI's position in education.

In a 2022 report, the World Economic Forum underlined an undeniable truth: the embrace of AI in education is uneven and skewed heavily in favor of high-income countries.[7] The COVID-19 pandemic accentuated existing disparities in education, highlighting the deep-rooted inequalities that exist within global schooling systems. The crisis brought to light the significant challenges and uneven access to educational resources, affecting students from varied socioeconomic backgrounds.

From the United States to China, the United Kingdom to India, nations are pumping billions into AI education, driven by the recognition of AI's pivotal role in sculpting future economies. They're betting big, convinced that AI in education will pay dividends. It's a high-stakes game, one that's reshaping education as we know it.

Yet, the undeniable fact remains that the strides made in AI in education are inconsistent across the globe, often dictated by fluctuating socioeconomic trends and seismic shifts in policy and technology. These disparities underscore the urgent need for concerted global efforts to ensure AI in education doesn't remain the privilege of a select few but becomes a universal right. It's a challenge we must rise to meet because the future of education – and perhaps even of our world – depends on it.

The Flipside of the Coin: Unmasking AI Education's Hidden Pitfalls

AI's march into the education sector is not without its challenges, promising precision and performance, but also prone to certain irrefutable frailties.

The first stumbling block lies in AI's inability to mimic the intricacies of human interaction and mentorship, a reality that the remote learning era ushered in by the COVID-19 pandemic hammered home. The *New York Academy of Sciences*, in a landmark study conducted in 2021, unearthed a compelling truth – students, when cradled by a supportive mentor, displayed an amplified passion for learning. Human teachers, with their capacity to foster emotional intelligence, empathy, and creativity, are the indispensable linchpins of the education system, reminding us that AI can aid, but not replace, the human touch.[8]

The digital divide remains a significant challenge in the landscape of AI-driven education. The 2021 report from the US National Center for Education Statistics highlights that 12 percent of American children aged three to eighteen lacked home internet access, a problem exacerbated during the COVID-19 pandemic's shift to online education.[9] Globally, the situation is even more stark, with a 2020 UNICEF report indicating that two-thirds of school-aged children worldwide lack digital access.[10] This disparity limits the reach of AI educational tools, making them a privilege accessible primarily to those in well-resourced areas.

Alongside the digital divide, the specter of privacy infringement haunts the realm of AI education. With AI-driven education platforms mushrooming throughout the 2010s, student data started to pile up, triggering alarms about safety. A 2022 study by Human Rights Watch found a gaping hole in the protective shield around student data, with a considerable 89 percent of educational technology vendors failing to meet minimum privacy and security standards.[11]

This privacy storm stirred global waters. Countries, including those bound by the European Union's General Data Protection Regulation (GDPR), clamped down on data collection and processing with strict rules. In 2021, China entered the fray with its Personal Information Protection Law (PIPL), reinforcing the international reach of the privacy concerns marring AI-led education.[12]

The exciting promises of AI education, therefore, must be tempered with a healthy dose of reality. We must reckon with the need for human mentorship in a tech-driven education landscape, dismantle the barriers of the digital divide to ensure equitable access, and throw a security blanket over student data in an age when privacy is a diminishing commodity.

These hurdles and their solutions are driven by significant global events, revealing the fluid and ever-changing nature of education in the digital era. The watch continues to tick, and we must ensure that the allure of AI education does not eclipse its potential perils.

AI and Personalized Learning: Education's New Frontier or Fool's Gold?

Once upon a time, education's Holy Grail was a one-size-fits-all approach, herding learners of all stripes into a homogeneous curriculum. But like any relic of the past, it became outdated and cumbersome. Welcome to the new dawn – personalized learning, powered by artificial intelligence, promising to turn the creaking gears of traditional education into a sleek machine. But as the tale unfolds, one can't help but ask – is this really a fresh horizon or a castle built on sand?

AI in education operates in a world where every child is unique, deserving a learning journey tailored just to them. RAND Corporation's 2017 study offers a tantalizing glimpse into this future. Schools with AI-guided personalized learning systems are outpacing traditional classrooms, adding up to four months of additional progress in mathematics and reading.[13]

AI's star pupils include the likes of Knewton and DreamBox Learning, with their claims of near-miraculous advancements. Knewton, an adaptive-learning platform, is like a personal tutor, scrutinizing each student's performance, identifying learning gaps, and molding content to fill them. And it didn't just stop at promises. Between 2012 and 2015, Knewton reported a 17 percent rise in pass rates.[14]

Meanwhile, DreamBox Learning, an AI-infused math program, is busy reshaping young minds. Not only does it adapt learning content on the fly but it also delivers powerful insights to teachers, enabling them to intervene effectively when students falter. A Harvard study in 2016 revealed that just fourteen hours of engagement with DreamBox boosted standardized math test scores by a notable 5.5 percent.[15]

Other AI prodigies, like Carnegie Learning's MATHia and Duolingo, are joining the fray, each with their unique spin on AI-driven personalized learning. Duolingo, the multilingual application, equates thirty-four hours on its platform to a full university semester, a bold claim buoyed by its 300 million strong user base in 2020.[16]

But in this exciting new era, AI needs to consider more than just academic success. It needs to delve into the minds of learners, factoring in their motivation, emotions, and passions. A paper in the *International Journal of Child-Computer Interaction* echoed this sentiment in 2022, pushing for AI systems that account for learners' emotional states to keep the motivation furnace burning.[17]

So, is AI the knight in shining armor for personalized learning, riding in to democratize education? Or is it another cautionary tale of Silicon Valley excess, replete with inflated promises and unintended consequences? AI cuts both ways. Data privacy, overreliance on technology, and the specter of harmful biases lurk in the shadows of AI's shimmering promise. The more important question is, will AI eventually render universities obsolete? It is challenging to provide a direct answer to this complex question. AI has the potential to transform higher education by providing personalized learning experiences and making education more accessible. However, it is unlikely to replace the comprehensive role of universities. Universities offer more than just knowledge dissemination; they provide mentorship, research opportunities, social development, and a structured learning environment. AI can enhance these aspects but cannot fully replicate the multifaceted experience and community that universities offer. Therefore, while AI will significantly impact how education is delivered, it's more likely to complement rather than replace traditional universities.

As this tale of AI and personalized learning unfolds, the jury is still out. Are we truly on the cusp of a learning revolution, or is this another rush for fool's gold? Only time will tell if AI will carve out a place in the annals of education or end up as a footnote in its history.

AI and Special Education: A Narrative of Trials and Triumph

In the daunting labyrinth of special education, every child's journey is a solitary path, strewn with singular challenges and victories. Artificial intelligence has entered the arena of education, presenting both significant opportunities for innovation and notable challenges to address.

Imagine a child grappling with dyslexia, the letters on the page eluding their grasp like shadows. AI-based speech recognition, embedded in tools like

Google's Voice Typing and Microsoft's Dictate, transforms this landscape. Suddenly, the written word is not a herculean task but a friend, waiting to take form from the spoken language. A 2022 Education and Information Technologies study echoes this optimism, documenting that dyslexic students using dictation software showed tangible improvements in their writing tasks.[18]

In another corner of this intricate world, visually impaired students find their classrooms expanding, courtesy of Microsoft's Seeing AI. This nifty app significantly enhances these students' learning environment. Acting as a digital guide, this app interprets visual information in real time; reads texts aloud, describing people, objects, and scenes. This technology empowers visually impaired students with greater independence, allowing them to engage more fully with their educational materials and classroom activities. It effectively expands their learning experience beyond traditional boundaries, facilitating greater accessibility and interaction with their academic surroundings.[19]

The curtain rises further to reveal the stage of educational robots, and one robot named Milo holds the spotlight. This brainchild of RoboKind, Milo is an intriguing mix of AI and humanlike traits, tailored for students on the autism spectrum. Milo's consistent expressions and lessons give these students a reliable ally in their journey to learn social skills. A pilot study in *Science Robotics* in 2018 lent credence to Milo's effectiveness, noting improved social behavior and engagement among the participants.[20]

While integrating AI into special education holds promise, its successful implementation is not straightforward. It requires a nuanced approach where educators and parents play a critical role. The 2022 book *Experimental Studies in Learning Technology and Child–Computer Interaction* emphasizes the importance of educators in guiding the use of AI. It highlights that for students with special needs to fully benefit from AI technologies, teachers must be actively involved in selecting and applying these tools effectively in the learning environment.[21]

The realm of special education, thus, sees a new dawn in AI, a horizon brimming with possibilities of personalized and inclusive learning. It's not without its stormy skies – the interplay between human guidance and AI's potential will determine if we see the rainbow at the end. The challenge lies in harnessing AI to empower rather than overpower, to illuminate rather than overshadow the educational journeys of those with special needs. This is a delicate dance, and its rhythm will shape the future of special education.

An Eye to the Future: Navigating the AI in Education Landscape

As we venture further into the twenty-first century, the use of AI in education is projected to snowball. Global Market Report, in an incisive report, predicts that AI in the education market will catapult to a remarkable $30 billion by

2032.[22] This underscores the imperative of integrating AI judiciously, ensuring it serves as an aide-de-camp to traditional education, rather than an overbearing usurper.

In adapting to AI in education, the role of teachers is evolving. They are increasingly becoming facilitators who guide students in using AI tools effectively. This shift involves focusing on developing skills like creativity, critical thinking, and emotional intelligence, which AI cannot fully replicate. Teachers' expertise in these human-centric areas remains crucial, ensuring that education maintains its core values while integrating technological advancements. This approach leverages AI's capabilities to enhance learning while preserving the essential human elements of teaching.

The advent of AI in education invites us to explore uncharted territories, where the promise of personalization and efficiency stretches out as far as the eye can see. Yet, we must be cautious in our approach, understanding that the full power of AI can only be harnessed when it is deftly woven into the tapestry of teaching and learning. Technology will continue its inexorable march forward, but at the heart of education lies a profoundly human enterprise.

In navigating the integration of AI in education, it's crucial to find a balance between machine efficiency and human creativity. This balance is key to creating an educational environment that is both inclusive and effective, leveraging AI for its strengths while valuing the irreplaceable aspects of human interaction. Achieving this harmony not only is beneficial for current learning environments but will also set a foundational legacy for future generations of learners.

References

1 "Knewton Is Building the World's Smartest Tutor," accessed September 5, 2023, https://www.forbes.com/sites/bruceupbin/2012/02/22/knewton-is-building-the-worlds-smartest-tutor/?sh=26df157717a7.
2 Opinium (firm) (2019). "The 2019 Teacher Digital Perspectives Survey." https://www.et-foundation.co.uk/wp-content/uploads/2019/06/2019-Teacher-Digital-Perspectives-Report.pdf
3 S. Wang, C. Christensen, W. Cui, R. Tong, L. Yarnall, L. Shear, and M. Feng (2023). "When Adaptive Learning Is Effective Learning: Comparison of an Adaptive Learning System to Teacher-Led Instruction," *Interactive Learning Environments*, 31(2), 793–803.
4 J. F. Pane, E. D. Steiner, M. D. Baird, and L. S. Hamilton (2015). *Continued Progress: Promising Evidence on Personalized Learning.* Santa Monica, CA: RAND Corporation. https://www.rand.org/pubs/research_reports/RR1365.html.
5 "Coursera Reports Fourth Quarter and Full-Year 2022 Financial Results," accessed September 5, 2023, https://investor.coursera.com/news/news-details/2023/Coursera-Reports-Fourth-Quarter-and-Full-Year-2022-Financial-Results/default.aspx.
6 "Byju's Revenue and Usage Statistics" (2023), accessed September 5, 2023, https://mobilemarketingreads.com/byjus-revenue-and-usage-statistics-2020/.
7 World Economic Forum (May 2022). "Education, C. 4.0. Investing in the Future of Learning for a Human-Centric Recovery," *Insight Report*, accessed September 5, 2023, https://www3.weforum.org/docs/WEF_Catalysing_Education_4.0_2022.pdf.

8 E. B. Raposa, M. Hagler, D. Liu, and J. E. Rhodes (2021). "Predictors of Close Faculty-Student Relationships and Mentorship in Higher Education: Findings from the Gallup–Purdue Index," *Annals of the New York Academy of Sciences*, 1483(1), 36–49.
9 National Center for Education Statistics (2023). "Children's Internet Access at Home, Condition of Education," *U.S. Department of Education, Institute of Education Sciences*, accessed September 5, 2023, https://nces.ed.gov/programs/coe/indicator/cch/home-internet-access.
10 "Two-Thirds of the World's School-Age Children Have No Internet Access at Home," *New UNICEF-ITU Report Says*, accessed September 5, 2023, https://www.unicef.org/press-releases/two-thirds-worlds-school-age-children-have-no-internet-access-home-new-unicef-itu.
11 "Online Learning Products Enabled Surveillance of Children," accessed September 5, 2023, https://www.hrw.org/news/2022/07/12/online-learning-products-enabled-surveillance-children.
12 "Translation: Personal Information Protection Law of the People's Republic of China – Effective November 1, 2021," *Stanford DigiChina*, accessed December 30, https://digichina.stanford.edu/work/translation-personal-information-protection-law-of-the-peoples-republic-of-china-effective-nov-1-2021/.
13 J. F. Pane, E. D. Steiner, M. D. Baird, L. S. Hamilton, and J. D. Pane (2017). *How Does Personalized Learning Affect Student Achievement?* Santa Monica, CA: RAND Corporation, https://www.rand.org/pubs/research_briefs/RB9994.html.
14 "Great Use Cases of Adaptive Learning in Education," accessed September 5, 2023, https://www.edtechreview.in/trends-insights/trends/adaptive-learning-in-education/.
15 "DreamBox Learning Achievement Growth in the Howard County Public School System and Rocketship Education" (2016), *Center for Education Policy at Harvard University*, accessed September 5, 2023, https://cepr.harvard.edu/publications/dreambox-learning-achievement-growth.
16 C. Freeman, A. Kittredge, H. Wilson, and B. Pajak (2023). *The Duolingo Method for App-Based Teaching and Learning*. Pittsburgh, PA: Duolingo, https://duolingo-papers.s3.amazonaws.com/reports/duolingo-method-whitepaper.pdf
17 F. K. Lehnert, J. Niess, C. Lallemand, P. Markopoulos, A. Fischbach, and V. Koenig (2022). "Child-Computer Interaction: From a Systematic Review Towards an Integrated Understanding of Interaction Design Methods for Children," *International Journal of Child-Computer Interaction*, 32, 100398.
18 A. Al-Dokhny, A. M. Bukhamseen, and A. M. Drwish (2022). "Influence of Assistive Technology Applications on Dyslexic Students: The Case of Saudi Arabia during the COVID-19 Pandemic," *Education and Information Technologies*, 27(9), 12213–12249.
19 "Artificial Intelligence in the Classroom," accessed September 5, 2023, https://edublog.microsoft.com/en-au/2019/01/artificial-intelligence-in-the-classroom/.
20 T. Belpacme, J. Kennedy, A. Ramachandran, B. Scassellati, and F. Tanaka (2018). "Social Robots for Education: A Review," *Science Robotics*, 3(21), eaat5954.
21 M. Giannakos (2022). "Learning Technology and Child–Computer Interaction," In J. M. Spector; M. J. Bishop; D. Ifenthaler (eds), *Experimental Studies in Learning Technology and Child-Computer Interaction* (pp. 7–14), Cham: Springer International Publishing.
22 "AI in Education Market Size (2023)," accessed September 5, 2023, https://www.gminsights.com/industry-analysis/artificial-intelligence-ai-in-education-market.

8 Charting a New Course

Universities Embrace the Digital Revolution

Against the backdrop of the ever-evolving technological landscape, higher education has become a frontier of rapid transformation. As we traverse the globe, we find universities deftly riding the wave of online and hybrid learning models, acknowledging their potential to broaden education's reach and inject a potent dose of flexibility into its framework.

Long before the COVID-19 pandemic became an unwelcome catalyst for change, an estimated 35 percent of college students in the United States were already enrolled in at least one online course, according to the National Center for Education Statistics. Fast forward to the tumultuous end of 2020, a noteworthy 90 percent of students had turned to some form of online learning.[1] Indeed, while this shift may seem staggering, it's crucial to recognize that this was less a choice and more a compulsory adaptation in response to the global crisis. With schools and universities across the globe shuttering their physical doors, online education emerged not just as an alternative but also as the only viable conduit for uninterrupted learning. Institutions like Harvard and MIT, with their established e-learning platforms such as edX, were well positioned to guide this necessary transition, offering a semblance of continuity in a world brimming with uncertainties. Amid the upheaval, stalwarts like Harvard and MIT had a steady hand, driving the e-learning trend with the pioneering platform edX. The expansive reach of edX is illustrated by its global student body that ballooned to over 34 million in 2023, as reported by Inside Higher Ed.[2]

The University of New South Wales (UNSW) in Australia was not to be left behind. With the launch of the digital Uplift program, UNSW displayed an agile response to the pandemic, transitioning more than 300 courses fully online in 2020.[3] The UNSW report lauded the initiative for preserving the continuity and quality of education during lockdowns, reaching 104,663 students across the globe.[4]

The Indian government, foreseeing the digital trend, championed e-learning with the SWAYAM (Study Webs of Active Learning for Young Aspiring

DOI: 10.4324/9781003476504-9

Minds) initiative in 2017. The program bore the fruits of this forward-thinking approach when, by 2023, more than 2,000 online courses from high school to postgraduation level had seen a remarkable 13 million enrollments, as stated by India's Ministry of Education.[5]

Meanwhile, Tsinghua University in China marked its spot on the e-learning map with the "Rain Classroom," a distinctive online learning platform that had already catered to more than 3.27 million monthly active users by 2019.[6] Recognized by *China Daily* as a trailblazer in democratizing education, the university set a precedent for other institutions in the country. Akin to this, Keio University in Japan formed a strategic alliance with FutureLearn, an international online learning platform, in 2015. Such collaboration catapulted Keio University's academic influence globally, reaching 100,000 course registrants in 2023.[7]

As we scan the global educational landscape, it's evident that online and hybrid learning models are molding a new educational reality. By venturing beyond their campuses, universities are reshaping the blueprint of access to education and maintaining an unbroken thread of learning, even in the most trying times. The steady enrollment upsurge and the ringing endorsements from students and educators bear testament to the efficacy of these innovative models.

Universities Forge Industry Partnerships

As we continue our journey through the evolving higher education landscape, a striking trend emerges. Universities are increasingly forming partnerships with industry players, a move aimed at enhancing student readiness for the workforce. These alliances involve collaboration on curriculum development, providing internships and co-op programs, and bringing industry experts into the classroom. The goal is to equip students with practical skills and experience that are directly applicable in their future careers, thus narrowing the gap between academic learning and real-world application. This strategy also helps universities stay current with industry trends and needs, ensuring their programs remain relevant and valuable in the job market.

In the bustling city-state of Singapore, the SkillsFuture Work-Study Degree Programs set a compelling example, creating a symbiotic relationship between academia and the real world. By 2022, this initiative had witnessed a steadfast growth, both in its scale and influence, with the program catalog now boasting more than 190 work-study courses that have fostered the talents and skills of approximately 9,000 beneficiaries.[8]

However, it's the aftermath of these programs that truly validates their worth. A 2022 report by the Ministry of Education, Singapore, revealed an impressive 95.87 percent of NUS work-study participants landing full-time jobs within six months of graduating, underscoring the value of this industry-academia partnership.[9,10]

A similar narrative unfolded in South Korea, the policy programs for promoting joint University-Industry have been initiated by the government since 2007. The programs' dual mission was clear: to foster industry-oriented research and to facilitate internships for students, thereby providing a practical edge to their learning. As per a 2009 report by The Korea Association of Industry, Academy and Research Institute, the policy program has funded 44,004 million won (36.7 million US dollars) to 1,207 selected projects, with each receiving an average of 36.5 million won (30,000 US dollars).[11]

An innovative approach unfolded on the African continent, where Stellenbosch University unveiled LaunchLab in 2015. This unique business incubator links eager students with industry partners, incubating startups in the process. By 2023, LaunchLab had successfully incubated more than 200 startups, created more than 500 jobs, and raised in excess of ZAR 450 million (24 million USD) in seed funding.[12] This promising record provides a tangible demonstration of how universities can contribute directly to economic growth and job creation.

These groundbreaking initiatives illuminate the manifold advantages of university-industry partnerships. For students, the partnerships present a golden opportunity to test academic theories against the unforgiving realities of the business world, thereby enhancing their employability. For industries, the partnerships offer an influx of fresh perspectives and cutting-edge research, kindling the flame of innovation. For the universities, the alliances can elevate their stature, draw superior student talent, and unlock new funding avenues via industry-sponsored research.

Tectonic Shifts: Chronicles of Technology's Siege on Higher Education

As we delve into the tempestuous yet captivating world of higher education, a revolution is quietly taking root. Virtual reality (VR) and augmented reality (AR) – once the playthings of Silicon Valley visionaries – have now seeped into the hallowed halls of academia. By 2030, VR and AR could command a significant $56.4 billion chunk of the education market, as projected by a verified market research report in 2022.[13]

Stanford University, ever the avant-garde innovator, has plunged into this new ground headfirst. Their Virtual Human Interaction Lab leverages VR to guide students through realms inaccessible to the naked eye, revealing climate change's creeping terror or the labyrinthine complexity of the human body.[14]

A 1,000 miles away, Case Western Reserve University is charting a similar path. In an unprecedented alliance with tech behemoth Microsoft, they're using HoloLens technology to train medical students, replacing dusty textbooks with three-dimensional human anatomical marvels.[15]

Parallel to the rise of VR and AR, a second revolution is stirring: artificial intelligence. This shape-shifter technology is setting the stage for personalized learning, automated assessments, and data-driven insights. Forecasts from Research and Market suggest an almost meteoric ascent for AI in education – a compound annual growth rate of over 10 percent from 2023 to 2032.[16]

Venturing further into 2023, the integration of artificial intelligence in education is transcending its initial novelty to become a multifaceted tool for enhancing learning experiences. While the rapid growth of AI in education reflects its increasing significance, the landscape is evolving with nuanced developments. Recent insights highlight that AI's greatest impacts in education are seen in areas like content preparation, assessment, and personalized learning. Teachers globally acknowledge the positive influence of AI-powered technology on educational outcomes, with a significant majority finding it beneficial in various aspects of teaching and learning.

Furthermore, in the context of EdTech trends for 2023, AI's role is pivotal. It's not just shaping traditional learning outcomes, such as improving public-speaking skills through real-time feedback on virtual platforms, but also addressing aspects like student mental health and emotional intelligence. AI-based EdTech solutions are aiding in personalized stress-reduction techniques and fostering social interaction among students. This shift toward a learner-centric approach in EdTech, where the focus is more on "learning than schooling," underscores the transformative potential of AI in education.

At the forefront of this evolution stands Carnegie Mellon University. Their Open Learning Initiative, an AI-powered endeavor, offers students real-time feedback and custom resources while providing educators with crucial student performance data.[17] The University of Michigan has joined the vanguard too, with its AI-enabled GradeCraft tool, a gamified learning platform helping students navigate their learning journeys.[18]

Additionally, the Stanford Institute for Human-Centered Artificial Intelligence's 2023 AI Index provides a broader perspective. It reveals a significant increase in large language models' scale, the need for new benchmarks to challenge advancing AI tools, and the heightened environmental costs of training large models.[19] These developments suggest that as AI becomes more integral to education, its ethical, environmental, and technical challenges must also be addressed, ensuring responsible and sustainable implementation.

AI in education is no longer just a burgeoning field but a dynamic ecosystem undergoing rapid evolution and expansion. Its impact spans from enhancing personalized learning experiences to posing new challenges in terms of ethics, environmental sustainability, and teacher preparedness. This multifaceted progression of AI in education is setting the stage for a more inclusive, effective, and future-ready learning environment.

Finally, we arrive at the dawn of a blockchain revolution in credential validation. Leading the charge is the University of Basel in Switzerland, testing the waters with a pilot program for issuing blockchain-encrypted diplomas.[20] This move could singlehandedly dismantle the plague of fraudulent academic credentials, creating an efficient, ironclad verification system.

Meanwhile, the University of Nicosia in Cyprus has blazed a trail as the first university worldwide to issue blockchain certificates. By 2021, they'd achieved a complete transformation of their degree-issuance process, handing students their instantly accessible credentials on a blockchain platter.[21]

The American Council on Education's report paints an intriguing future, forecasting that by 2025, one in five universities will have embraced blockchain for credentialing.[22]

In this ongoing story of technology's march through academia, VR, AR, AI, and blockchain are pivotal elements. The transformations they promise – richly immersive teaching, tailor-made learning, and foolproof credentials – may well redraw the contours of higher education.

Navigating the Digital Storm: A New Era of Leadership in Higher Education

Bounded by age-old hierarchies and traditions, the world of higher education leadership has often been likened to a slow, gentle river, meandering through time. However, with the advent of the digital age, this river now faces the fierce currents of technological change. A tsunami of new technologies, surging demands for lifelong learning, and a shifting educational landscape are forging a path that university leaders must now navigate.

A 2021 study by the *International Journal of Educational Technology in Higher Education*, titled "Digital higher education: a divider or bridge builder? Leadership perspectives on edtech in a COVID-19 reality," examines the significant changes in leadership styles within higher education. The report highlights how leaders in academia are increasingly adopting roles as facilitators of digital innovation. They are shifting from traditional, authoritative positions to being more adaptable, enthusiastic, and inspiring in guiding their institutions through technological advancements and changes in the educational landscape.[23]

In this innovative horizon, Arizona State University (ASU) has risen as a beacon of technological progress. Under the stewardship of President Michael Crow, ASU has embraced the digital revolution. This isn't your grandfather's ivory tower; ASU has opened the gates to the future with pioneering adaptive-learning technologies, a full-fledged online degree program, and synergistic alliances with corporations and community colleges. With each digital stride, ASU broadens its reach, creating ripples of educational opportunities.[24]

In the East, Singapore Management University (SMU) is carving out its digital path under the watchful eyes of President Lily Kong. As part of its Smart-Campus Initiative, SMU is harnessing the power of digital innovation to build a campus of the future, replete with personalized learning, enhanced faculty-student engagement, and improved administrative efficiency. The result – a thriving ecosystem that feeds on innovation.[25]

However, in this digital age, progress comes with a dark shadow – cybersecurity. As universities open the floodgates to digital technologies, they unwittingly expose themselves to a new breed of cyber-predators. A disconcerting revelation from a 2020 *EDUCAUSE Review* report highlights the significant cybersecurity threats facing educational institutions, emphasizing the increasing prevalence and sophistication of ransomware attacks in the higher education sector.[26] The stage is set for a cybersecurity showdown.

Seeing the writing on the wall, the University of California system is bracing for impact. In its defense, a Cyber-Risk Governance Committee acts as a sentinel, scanning the horizon for threats and fortifying the university's security. This cyber-watchdog is on a mission – to define the institution's risk appetite, safeguard its precious assets, shape and deploy robust cybersecurity strategies, and enforce a code of cyber-conduct.[27]

The dawn of the digital age signals a leadership crossroads for higher education. The leaders who succeed will be those who harness the power of digital innovation to enhance learning, research, and access while also standing guard against the lurking cyber-threats. In this digital storm, leadership is not just about steering the ship but also about weathering the storm.

Charting Unconventional Paths

In the realm of higher education transformation, innovation is the buzzword. Although "magic solutions" are the stuff of fiction, a slew of unique and pioneering initiatives have demonstrated noteworthy promise, challenging the status quo.

Halfway around the globe, the University of Otago embarked on a pioneering venture in New Zealand's academic landscape by introducing micro-credentials in health, education, and business in 2019. These programs, crafted in collaboration with industry experts, sought to offer professionals adaptable and pertinent educational opportunities. Student completion of these courses soared from 1,027 to 3,098, marking a 201 percent increase. Additionally, the number of such credentials listed in the New Zealand Qualifications Framework grew from twenty-seven to eighty-three. This expansion, driven by evolving educational needs amid global shifts like the COVID-19 pandemic and technological advancements, underscores the rising importance of targeted, skills-based education.[28,29]

In the realm of higher education, micro-credentials have emerged as a beacon of progress. Their benefits, as illuminated in scholarly discourse, lie in offering tailored learning experiences that enhance employability and bridge the skill gaps in the evolving job market. Yet, the journey is not without its hurdles. Ensuring the ongoing relevance and quality of these micro-credentials, alongside the task of seamlessly integrating them within the established educational frameworks, presents a challenge that educators and policymakers must navigate with care and insight.[29,30]

This shift toward micro-credentialing isn't an isolated phenomenon. Universities globally are gradually recognizing and integrating their significance. A 2023 report by the HolonIQ noted that over 30 percent of surveyed universities had incorporated some form of micro-credentialing, opening avenues for students and professionals to stay abreast of emerging skills and industry pivots.[31]

As we wrap up this chapter, one thing is clear: universities worldwide are steadfastly adopting digitalization, strengthening industry collaborations, and venturing into uncharted territories with innovative solutions. Yes, formidable challenges remain, but the overall trajectory is unwavering – a decisive pivot toward a more adaptable, skill-focused, and accessible future for higher education.

While there are no "magic solutions," universities' strategic initiatives show great potential in preparing students for a rapidly evolving world. Higher education is experiencing a continuous narrative of transformation, adapting to meet future educational demands and challenges. This dynamic process is reflective of the changing higher-education landscape, with institutions constantly revising their strategies to keep pace with global trends and workforce needs. The evolution of universities is a continuous journey, one that consistently adapts to meet the demands of the future. This transformative process, fueled by innovation and resilience, plays a crucial role in preparing the next generation for success and fulfillment in a rapidly changing world.

Navigating the Future: The Evolution of Higher Education

As we cast our gaze into the future, universities' progressive adaptation to a relentlessly digital and interconnected world seems irrefutable. The footprint of online and hybrid learning models is projected to expand, fueled by leaps in technology and an escalating acknowledgment of their efficacy and scalability. Predicting the exact proportion of future online learners presents a significant challenge. Yet, a report by *Inside Higher Ed* revealed a significant increase in the number of students enrolled exclusively in fully online programs, jumping from 3.5 million to 5.8 million in a specified twelve-month period (2020–21), which represents a rise from 17.6 percent to 22.7 percent of all students engaging in online learning.[32]

In a world where professional readiness is increasingly paramount, expect the fusion of academia and industry to intensify. Universities are likely to perceive these partnerships less as "value-added" facets and more as integral cogs driving curriculum structure and content. The World Economic Forum forecasts that by 2025, a significant 50 percent of all university students will be engaged in work-study programs or internships as part of their degree curriculum.[33]

On the front of educational innovation, initiatives like the AI for Everyone and micro-credentialing, currently seen as unique, are poised to become the norm. Universities' continued attempts to align their curriculum with fluctuating industry requirements will necessitate such initiatives. With AI and other advanced technologies tightening their grip on the future, expect a more extensive gamut of courses tailored to emerging technologies and societal necessities.

However, amid the promising developments, the accompanying challenges are unavoidable. Hurdles such as the digital divide, equitable access to resources, student data privacy, and the effectiveness of online learning demand relentless scrutiny and refinement. Therefore, the coming times won't merely be about rolling out novel strategies but refining them continuously to ensure an inclusive, quality higher education for all.

The repositioning of universities is anything but a static process. It demands perpetual learning, adaptation, and a bold willingness to unsettle traditional models. Nevertheless, given the spirit of innovation and an unwavering commitment to student success that universities have displayed thus far, the horizon of higher education seems bright, standing resiliently prepared to face the evolving challenges of the twenty-first century.

References

1 "Percentage of Students in the United States Taking Distance Learning Courses from 2012 to 2021," accessed September 5, 2023, https://www.statista.com/statistics/944245/student-distance-learning-enrollment-usa/.
2 "Whatever Happened to MIT and Harvard's Big EdX Profit?" accessed September 5, 2023, https://www.insidehighered.com/news/tech-innovation/digital-teaching-learning/2023/04/28/whatever-happened-mit-and-harvards-big.
3 "From Digital Uplift to Educational Solutions," accessed September 5, 2023, https://www.education.unsw.edu.au/news/du-to-educational-solutions-support.
4 "Professor Ian Jacobs' Legacy for Academic Excellence at UNSW Sydney," accessed September 5, 2023, https://www.inside.unsw.edu.au/academic-excellence/professor-ian-jacobs-legacy-academic-excellence-unsw-sydney.
5 "Study Webs of Active Learning for Young Aspiring Minds (SWAYAM)," accessed September 5, 2023, https://swayam.gov.in/nc_details/.
6 X. Feng, K. Mi, Y. Shen, H. Hua, Y. Bian, and H. Bian (2022). "Rain Classroom Assisted by WeChat for Preliminary Online Physiology Teaching during the COVID-19 Pandemic," *Advances in Physiology Education*, 46(2), 319–324.
7 "Free Online Courses on FutureLearn: Keio University's Open Courses Achieve 100,000 Registrants," accessed September 5, 2023, https://www.keio.ac.jp/en/press-releases/2023/Sep/8/49-151781/.
8 "Four New SkillsFuture Work-Study Programmes to Be Launched in 2023," accessed September 5, 2023, https://www.skillsfuture.gov.sg/newsroom/four-new-skillsfuture-work-study-programmes-to-be-launched-in-2023.
9 "Graduate Employment Survey," accessed September 10, 2023, https://www.moe.gov.sg/-/media/files/post-secondary/ges-2022/web-publication-nus-ges-2022.ashx.
10 "SkillsFuture Work-Study Degree," accessed September 10, 2023, https://www.skillsfuture.gov.sg/workstudy/wsdeg.
11 K. R. Lee (2014). "University-Industry R&D Collaboration in Korea's National Innovation System," *Science, Technology and Society*, 19(1), 1–25.

12 "LaunchLab Stellenbosch University," accessed September 10, 2023, https://www.launchlab.co.za/.
13 "Global Augmented and Virtual Reality In Education Market Size by Offering (Solutions, Services), by Deployment Model (Cloud, On-Premises), by Application (K–12, Higher Education), by Geographic Scope and Forecast," accessed September 10, 2023, https://www.verifiedmarketresearch.com/product/augmented-and-virtual-reality-in-education-market/.
14 "Virtual Human Interaction Lab," *Stanford University Virtual Human Interaction Lab*, accessed December 30, https://vhil.stanford.edu/.
15 "HoloAnatomy® Software Suite," *Case Western Reserve University*, accessed December 30, https://case.edu/holoanatomy/.
16 "AI in Education Market Size—By Component (Solution, Service), by Deployment (On-premise, Cloud), by Technology (Machine Learning, Deep Learning, Natural Language Processing), Application, End-Use and Forecast, 2023–2032," *Global Market Insights*, accessed September 14, 2023, https://www.gminsights.com/industry-analysis/artificial-intelligence-ai-in-education-market.
17 "Open Learning Initiative," *Carnegie Mellon University*, accessed December 16, 2023, https://oli.cmu.edu/.
18 "GradeCraft," *University of Michigan*, accessed September 14, 2023, https://ai.umich.edu/software-applications/gradecraft/.
19 "Stanford Institute for Human-Centered Artificial Intelligence (2023)," *AI Index Report 2023*, accessed December 16, 2023, https://aiindex.stanford.edu/report/.
20 "Blockchain Diploma," *Faculty of Business and Economics, University of Basel*, accessed December 30, https://wwz.unibas.ch/en/dltfintech/blockchain-diploma/.
21 "University of Nicosia. Blockchain Programs," accessed December 16, 2023, https://www.unic.ac.cy/blockchain-programs/.
22 N. Smolenski (2021). "Blockchain for Education: A New Credentialing Ecosystem," *OECD Digital Education Outlook 2021 Pushing the Frontiers with Artificial Intelligence, Blockchain and Robots*, p. 209, accessed December 16, 2023, https://blogs.ugto.mx/mdued/wp-content/uploads/sites/66/2022/09/OECD-Digital-Education-Outlook-2021.pdf.
23 R. M. Fisher and H. Leder (2022). "An Assessment of Micro-Credentials in New Zealand Vocational Education," *International Journal of Training Research*, 20(3), 232–247.
24 M. Laufer, A. Leiser, B. Deacon, P. Perrin de Brichambaut, B. Fecher, C. Kobsda, and F. Hesse (2021). "Digital Higher Education: A Divider or Bridge Builder? Leadership Perspectives on Edtech in a COVID-19 Reality," *International Journal of Educational Technology in Higher Education*, 18, 1–17.
25 "20 Years in: A Look at President Crow's Vision for Accessibility and Excellence in the New American University," *ASU News Article*, accessed December 30, https://news.asu.edu/20221123-arizona-impact-20-years-look-president-crows-vision-accessibility-and-excellence-new.
26 "SMU President Professor Lily Kong Shares Her Vision of a University," *Singapore Management University Newsroom*, accessed December 30, https://news.smu.edu.sg/news/2021/07/10/smu-president-professor-lily-kong-shares-her-vision-university.
27 S. Scholz, B. Hagen, and C. Lee (2021). "The Increasing Threat of Ransomware in Higher Education," *EDUCAUSE Review*, accessed April 13, 2022, https://er.educause.edu/articles/2021/6/the-increasingthreat-of-ransomware-in-higher-education.
28 "Shared Governance," *University of California*, accessed December 30, https://security.ucop.edu/about/cyber-risk-governance/shared-governance.html.
29 "Micro-Credential Approval, Accreditation and Listing," *New Zealand Qualifications Authority*, accessed December 16, 2023, https://www2.nzqa.govt.nz/tertiary/approval-accreditation-and-registration/micro-credentials/.

30 T. Neal, G. Klinkum, L. Reid, and N. Miller (2022). "Aotearoa New Zealand's Early Micro-Credentials Journey: Insights Paper," *New Zealand Qualifications*. https://www2.nzqa.govt.nz/assets/About-us/Publications/Insights-papers/Micro-credentials/Aotearoa-New-Zealands-early-micro-credentials-journey.pdf
31 "Micro Credentials Survey, 2023 Trends and Insights," *HolonIQ*, accessed September 14, 2023, https://www.holoniq.com/notes/micro-credentials-survey-2023-insights.
32 "New U.S. Data Show Jump in College Students' Learning Online," *Inside Higher Ed*, accessed September 14, 2023, https://www.insidehighered.com/news/2021/10/13/new-us-data-show-jump-college-students-learning-online#:~:text=The percent-20number percent20of percent20students percent20enrolled,be percent20enrolled percent20in percent20thoses.
33 "The Future of Jobs Report 2020," accessed July 30, 2023, https://weforum.org/reports/the-future-of-jobs-report-2020/.

9 University in 3-D
Academia, Society, and Personal Growth

Turning Individuals into Global Citizens

University years are a critical phase of transformation for young adults. Beyond the formal education and pursuit of academic degrees, universities shape students' political, ethical, and societal viewpoints, often helping them evolve from individuals into global citizens.

Consider the political landscape. The multiyear study by the Higher Education Research Institute at UCLA indicates that university students tend to adopt more liberal views over time, often influenced by their exposure to diverse perspectives and experiences.[1] However, this raises an important question in the era of increasing online learning: does the virtual environment offer the same breadth of personal interaction necessary for this kind of ideological shift? While online platforms provide access to a wide range of viewpoints, the absence of physical campus interactions might limit students' exposure to the diverse personal experiences that often catalyze changes in perspective. This concern underscores the need for educational institutions to actively foster interactive and diverse online communities, ensuring that the shift to digital learning continues to promote an understanding and acceptance of different backgrounds and ideas.

Universities also play an integral part in igniting the flame of civic duty and community involvement. The National Study of Learning, Voting, and Engagement, in its 2019 report, found that student voting rates at participating US universities had doubled between the 2014 and 2018 midterm elections.[2] This statistic underscores the transformative effect of a university experience in instilling a sense of civic responsibility among students.

Shaping Identity, Fostering Resilience

From a personal development standpoint, universities serve as experimental grounds for students to explore and define their identities. Erik Erikson, in his influential work on psychosocial development (1968), posited that young adults grapple with a crisis between identity and role confusion.[3] Universities, offering a rich tapestry of experiences and opportunities, provide the perfect setting for this identity exploration.

For example, study-abroad programs expose students to a kaleidoscope of cultural experiences. According to a 2020 report by NAFSA: Association of International Educators, more than 341,000 American students had the opportunity to study abroad in the 2017–18 academic year.[4] These cross-cultural encounters do more than enrich students' understanding of the world; they also foster resilience and adaptability – traits highly valued in our increasingly globalized world.

Universities also offer a stage for leadership development. According to a 2018 survey from the Multi-Institutional Study of Leadership, participation in leadership programs significantly boosted students' self-efficacy and commitment to societal change. By allowing students to lead initiatives, manage projects, and work in diverse teams, universities foster a sense of self-confidence and purpose that extends beyond academia.[5]

In essence, the influence of universities transcends the boundaries of intellectual growth. Through their multifaceted roles, universities mold not just knowledgeable graduates but adaptable, resilient global citizens with a deep understanding of their responsibilities to society. This broader impact redefines the value of university education, painting it as a key ingredient in preparing students for a future filled with complex societal interactions and challenges.

Catalysts for Change: Universities in the Crucible of History

The reputation of universities as mere bastions of knowledge doesn't do justice to their rich history. They are, in essence, dynamic entities shaped by and shaping the societal landscape, from playing host to powerful movements of dissent to paving the path for individual metamorphosis.

Historically, universities have been at the forefront of major societal changes. In the 1960s, the University of California, Berkeley, emerged as a pivotal site for the Free Speech Movement. This student-led initiative in 1964 contested the control over public discourse, sparking national discussions on freedom of speech.

Simultaneously, universities in the Southern United States played a crucial role in the fight against racial segregation. A notable example was James Meredith's enrollment at the University of Mississippi in 1962. His entry into "Ole Miss" marked a significant moment in desegregating American higher education. Despite facing significant opposition, Meredith's actions paved the way for African American students, striking a significant blow against the barriers of racial segregation.[6]

During the Vietnam War era, universities were thrust into the spotlight again, serving as the battleground for antiwar protests. The infamous Kent

State shootings in 1970, where National Guardsmen opened fire on unarmed student protesters, killing four, were a stark testament to the tensions of the time. The fallout from this event – a nationwide student strike – resulted in the closure of hundreds of colleges and further inflamed public sentiment against the war.[7]

When we cast our gaze on the global stage, universities were instrumental in the anti-Apartheid movement of the 1980s. Scores of US and UK universities made the bold decision to divest from South Africa, applying economic and political pressure on the Apartheid regime. This action epitomized the universities' power to effect international change.[8]

The transformative power of universities extends to the individual, influencing not just academic growth but also personal development. Exposure to a range of thoughts, cultures, and experiences cultivates self-awareness, adaptability, and resilience.

The National Survey of Student Engagement's 2020 report offers an illuminating insight. The study, encompassing more than 500 institutions and thousands of students, revealed that half of the surveyed students credited their university experience for significant contributions to their self-understanding, self-esteem, and personal growth.[9]

The University of Minnesota further underscores this point through a 2018 study showing that students who had the opportunity to study abroad exhibited significant improvements in their intercultural competence, curiosity, and flexibility compared to their homebound peers.[10]

In essence, universities have been more than just academic institutions; they have served as catalysts for societal progression and individual growth. These seats of learning have played critical roles in shaping the discourse of our society, proving that the spirit of a university extends far beyond its lecture halls and into the heart of societal and personal transformation. As we delve into the impact of AI and technological changes in higher education, it's crucial to remember that universities' ultimate goal is not just academic excellence but also contributing to societal progress and personal transformation.

The Invisible Loss: When Nonacademic Elements Fade

The nonacademic facets of university life – cultural immersion, social interaction, and personal exploration – are as integral to a student's development as the academic curriculum. Their disappearance could precipitate significant deficiencies in the educational experience, impacting personal growth and long-term prospects for students.

The vibrant cultural mosaic of a university campus cannot be replicated elsewhere. Interacting with a medley of cultures nurtures a sense of global citizenship and sensitivity toward cultural nuances. In a 2018 study published in the *Journal of International Students*, it was found that the presence of international students on campus notably bolstered domestic students' cultural competence and cognitive abilities.[11] Without such rich cultural exchanges, academic environments could become less diverse and less inclusive, and potentially constrain students' worldviews.

Social development in a university is not limited to classrooms; it extends to sports fields, club meetings, and student government bodies. These nonacademic spaces cultivate leadership, teamwork, and time management – skills that prove invaluable in both professional and personal domains. A 2019 study in the *Journal of Higher Education* reinforced the importance of these activities, demonstrating a significant correlation between student engagement in extracurricular activities and improved self-perception and interpersonal skills.[12] Their absence could leave students bereft of essential life skills.

The psychological ramifications of losing nonacademic support services, like counseling and mental health resources, can't be overstated. According to a 2021 report from the American College Health Association, about 60 percent of college students reported overwhelming anxiety, while 40 percent experienced depressive symptoms that affected their functionality.[13] Campus mental health resources are often their lifeline, helping them navigate personal and academic challenges. Without this support, students could be left adrift during a critical period of their lives.

The journey of self-discovery and exploration at university often shapes a student's career trajectory. A survey by the National Association of Colleges and Employers (2020) revealed that nearly 60 percent of students attributed their career choices to their experiences and interactions at university. The loss of such experiences could leave students with a degree, but uncertain about their career path.[14]

Put simply, losing the nonacademic elements of university life could spell a deficit in the holistic development of students, leading to a diminished worldview, poor interpersonal skills, reduced psychological support, and indecisiveness in career choices. The magic of a university experience lies in its unique blend of academic and nonacademic facets that mold well-rounded individuals, equipped and motivated to make their mark on society. Without these nonacademic elements, universities may risk becoming factories of knowledge without cultivating wisdom.

To counteract the loss of nonacademic experiences in university life, especially in an increasingly digital education landscape, universities can adopt several strategies. First, virtual platforms can be enhanced to simulate campus experiences, using interactive tools and technologies like virtual reality to create immersive social and cultural environments. Second, universities can organize online extracurricular activities, such as virtual clubs, guest lectures, and networking events that foster community and interpersonal skills. Collaboration tools can facilitate group projects and discussions, ensuring that students still engage in teamwork and peer learning. Additionally, universities can implement robust online support systems, including counseling and career guidance services, to offer psychological support and career planning assistance. By integrating these elements into their online offerings, universities can strive to provide a holistic educational experience that not only imparts knowledge but also cultivates wisdom and well-roundedness in students.

The Online Paradox: Can We Replicate the Full University Experience Digitally?

The rise of digital learning environments raises a compelling question: can they offer the same breadth and depth of experiences a traditional university setting does? It's one thing to deliver academic knowledge over a screen; it's another to foster the same level of personal growth and social engagement that a university campus does.

Online platforms are adept at delivering content, and they can even facilitate interaction. Yet, they currently struggle to mimic the intensity and quality of interpersonal connection found in face-to-face settings. Take, for instance, the domain of debates and group discussions. A study published in the *International Review of Research in Open and Distributed Learning* (2020) pointed out that while online debate forums can promote critical thinking, they frequently lack the immediacy and the nonverbal communication that comes with in-person discussions.[15] The subtleties of face-to-face communication – the glimmers in eyes, the shifts in tones and in body language – all crucial in honing students' social and communication skills, are conspicuously absent in an online setup.

Moreover, the rich tapestry of cultural experiences and the serendipity of diversity, which are woven into the very fabric of a traditional university experience, become less accessible in an online-only format. The chance encounters at the campus café, the animated exchanges at cultural events, the lessons learned from informal conversations with peers from different parts of the globe – these aspects are not easily translatable to a digital landscape.

The predicament extends to extracurricular activities. While some clubs and organizations have adapted to the online environment, others – particularly those that demand physical presence such as sports, theater, and certain community service activities – lose their essence when transposed to the virtual world. These activities are more than just hobbies; they are platforms for developing leadership, fostering teamwork, and forging a sense of community.

Yet, we cannot dismiss the potential of technology. Advancements like virtual reality and augmented reality hold promise for enhancing the quality of online social interactions. A 2022 study featured in the *International Journal of Educational Technology in Higher Education* shed light on the ability of VR to craft immersive learning experiences that foster a sense of social presence and engagement.[16] As technology continues to evolve, the gap between traditional and online university experiences could progressively narrow.

Innovative approaches to enrich the online learning experience are also being explored. Hybrid models that blend the flexibility of online learning with intermittent in-person residencies for social networking are being trialed. Universities are also investing in online student services, including virtual career counseling, mental health support, and interactive online student communities.

In conclusion, while replicating the full spectrum of the traditional university experience in a digital environment remains a daunting task, the future holds potential. Technology's relentless march, coupled with innovative educational strategies, could gradually transform digital learning landscapes. However, the immeasurable value of face-to-face interaction, cultural immersion, and active campus life underscores the importance of preserving and cherishing the holistic experience that traditional university settings offer.

The Invisible Hands: How Governments and Societies Shape Universities

Governments and societies wield substantial influence in nurturing the nonacademic dimensions of universities. Their reach extends to funding, policy-making, and public sentiment, shaping the university landscape in tangible ways.

Let's consider the role of government funding. Universities aren't just homes to students; they're incubators of innovation, carrying out research and development initiatives that propel society forward. These efforts frequently rely on public funding. A compelling case is presented in a report by the National Science Board (2020), highlighting that government-funded university research has fueled advancements in key sectors, including healthcare, telecommunications, and energy. From the development of life-saving drugs to breakthroughs in sustainable energy solutions, universities have made significant strides, backed by government funding.[17]

Moving to the policy arena, governments have the power to mold higher education through the legislative process. One landmark legislation in the United States is the Title IX regulation, enacted in 1972. This single piece of legislation transformed the landscape of higher education, safeguarding students from gender-based discrimination, and promoting equitable participation in sports, academics, and other university activities.[18] Through policies like these, governments can cultivate an environment that encourages dialogue, debate, and learning.

Society's perception of universities is another influential factor. When universities are recognized by society as more than mere academic institutions – when they are seen as catalysts for personal development, social engagement, and broad learning – it emboldens them to prioritize these elements.

Public advocacy and activism have the potential to prod universities into action, pushing them to endorse causes that resonate with societal needs. Take the environmental sustainability movement as an example. This global call for environmental responsibility has had profound impacts on university policies and curricula. Universities worldwide have taken strides to make their campuses greener, and programs focused on sustainability have sprouted across academic departments.

The role of alumni and private contributions cannot be overlooked either. These donations often breathe life into university initiatives, fueling scholarships, infrastructural improvements, and extracurricular activities. A 2021 report by the Council for Advancement and Support of Education underlined this critical role, noting that US colleges and universities amassed a noteworthy $49.5 billion in private donations in a single year.[19]

The hand of government and the voice of society are instrumental in shaping the nonacademic functions of universities. Through funding, legislative actions, societal advocacy, and generous contributions, they support universities in their pursuit of providing a holistic education. This nurturing environment prepares students not just for their careers but also for their roles as future leaders and active participants in societal progress.

A New Horizon: The Future of Universities

As we venture into the future, we face an educational landscape in flux, stirred by the rise of online learning. Yet, the essence of universities – a blend of academic learning, personal growth, and social development – holds steadfast.

The emergence of online education poses its own set of challenges. Digital platforms can, without a doubt, disseminate academic knowledge with remarkable efficiency. Still, they grapple with replicating the richness of personal and social development opportunities that come naturally within the traditional university settings. The textures of cultural immersion, the vibrancy of campus life, and the profound personal connections that universities foster are difficult to fully emulate in a virtual world.

But every challenge presents an opportunity. This shift toward online learning has unlocked avenues for innovation, creating new methods for delivering personal and social development experiences. From virtual reality applications that transport students into immersive learning environments to online student communities that bridge geographic divides, the advent of technology holds exciting potential.

The role of governments and societies will be more critical than ever. Their recognition and support for the multifaceted role of universities will be vital. It's not merely about academic pursuits; universities are vital contributors to societal progress, molding individuals who are well rounded, culturally competent, and ready to tackle the challenges of the future.

Universities play a profound role that transcends academic boundaries. They are a cornerstone of societal structures and a launchpad for personal development. Their historical importance is undisputed, and their relevance in the modern era remains unquestionable. The loss of their nonacademic elements would be a blow that could ripple across generations, underlining the urgency to preserve these roles amid an evolving educational landscape.

As we stand at the threshold of this new era, the challenge is clear. Universities, governments, and societies – we must work together to ensure that the holistic essence of university life endures, keeping pace with technological advances while holding on to the age-old values that have shaped leaders and innovators throughout history. To realize the vision of preserving the holistic nature of university education in a digital age, a collaborative effort is essential. Universities can initiate partnerships with tech companies to develop interactive online platforms that closely mimic the on-campus experience. These platforms could include virtual reality classrooms, augmented reality campus tours, and AI-driven mentorship programs. Additionally, governments can play a pivotal role by providing funding and policy support for research and development in educational technologies, as well as by incentivizing public-private partnerships in this field. Societies, including alumni networks and local communities, can contribute by offering virtual internships and mentorship opportunities and engaging in online university events, thereby ensuring that students have access to a wide range of real-world experiences and networking opportunities. This collective approach will not only keep the essence of university life intact but will also enrich it with new possibilities brought forth by technological advancements.

References

1 "Politically Divided: Annual Survey of First-Year College Students Reveals Deep Partisan Splits," accessed September 14, 2023, https://www.insidehighered.com/news/2017/05/01/report-indicates-first-year-students-are-more-politically-polarized-ever.
2 "National Study of Learning, Voting, and Engagement," accessed September 14, 2023, https://idhe.tufts.edu/nslve.
3 E. H. Erikson, *Identity Youth and Crisis (No. 7)* (New York: WW Norton & Company, 1968).
4 "Open Doors' Data Show Continued Increase in Numbers of Americans Studying Abroad," accessed September 14, 2023, https://www.insidehighered.com/news/2019/11/18/open-doors-data-show-continued-increase-numbers-americans-studying-abroad.
5 B. P. Correia-Harker and S. L., Hall, *Campus Recreation and Leadership Development: Pathways for Student and Community 0Transformation* (Corvallis, OR: NIRSA, 2019).
6 "James Meredith at Ole Miss," *History*, accessed December 16, 2023, https://www.history.com/topics/black-history/ole-miss-integration.
7 "The May 4 Shootings at Kent State University: The Search for Historical Accuracy," *Kent State University*, accessed December 16, 2023, https://www.kent.edu/may-4-historical-accuracy.
8 "Disinvestment from South Africa," *Wikipedia*, accessed December 30, https://en.wikipedia.org/wiki/Disinvestment_from_South_Africa.

9 "2020 National Survey of Student Engagement," accessed September 14, 2023, https://isa.ncsu.edu/surveys/studentalumni-surveys/national-survey-of-student-engagement-nsse/nsse2020/.
10 K. P. Nichols (2011). "Fostering Intercultural Competence through Study Abroad: A Gender-Based Analysis of Individual and Program Factors Influencing Development," accessed September 14, 2023, https://conservancy.umn.edu/handle/11299/119984.
11 K. Bista and C. Glass, eds. (2018). "Journal of International Students," *OJED/STAR*, Vol. 8, no. 1.
12 P. Buckley and P. Lee (2021). "The Impact of Extra-Curricular Activity on the Student Experience," *Active Learning in Higher Education*, 22(1), 37–48.
13 "Spring 2021 Reference Group Executive Summary," *American College Health Association*, accessed September 14, 2023, https://www.acha.org/documents/ncha/ACHA-NCHA_II_SPRING_2021_REFERENCE_GROUP_EXECUTIVE_SUMMARY.pdf.
14 "Career Decision-Making Difficulties: A National Study of College Seniors, National," *Association of Colleges and Employers*, accessed September 14, 2023, https://www.naceweb.org/uploadedfiles/files/2020/publication/executive-summary/career-decision-making-difficulties-a-national-study-of-college-seniors.pdf.
15 B. H. Olivier (2016). "The Impact of Contact Sessions and Discussion Forums on the Academic Performance of Open Distance Learning Students," *International Review of Research in Open and Distributed Learning*, 17(6), 75–88.
16 S. M. Noble, J. D. Saville, and L. L. Foster (2022). "VR as a Choice: What Drives Learners' Technology Acceptance?" *International Journal of Educational Technology in Higher Education*, 19(1), 6.
17 "Academic Research and Development," *National Science Board*, accessed October 10, 2023, https://ncses.nsf.gov/pubs/nsb20213.
18 "Title IX of the Education Amendments of 1972," U.S. Department of Health & Human Services, accessed October 10, 2023, https://www.hhs.gov/civil-rights/for-individuals/sex-discrimination/title-ix-education-amendments/index.html.
19 E. Kaplan, *Voluntary Support of Education: Key Findings from Data Collected for the 2020–21 Academic Fiscal Year for US Higher Education Institutions* (Washington, D.C: Council for Advancement and Support of Education, 2022).

10 Bracing for the Twenties
Challenges of the Decade

The Technological Avalanche

A wave of technological change, led by advancements in AI, automation, and digital learning, is transforming the educational landscape worldwide, from the Americas to Asia and Australia. This shift opens up vast opportunities for innovative learning but also poses significant challenges for universities. They face the crucial task of updating curricula and teaching methods to prepare students for a future workforce increasingly shaped by technology, blending modern demands with traditional educational values.

The AI shockwave radiating across the job market isn't a mere regional aftershock but a global earthquake. McKinsey's Crystal Ball, in its 2017 report, paints a daunting picture: by the time 2030 rolls around, 14 percent of the world's workforce might find themselves shunted into new occupational alleys courtesy of automation and AI.[1] It's a wake-up call that Asia-Pacific's education titans, namely, Australia, Japan, South Korea, China, and Singapore, are heeding by recalibrating higher education toward digitization.

Australia is at the forefront, embarking on a campaign nudging its universities to tailor their offerings to the job trends of tomorrow. A clarion call from the Australian government's National Innovation and Science Agenda (2015) urges educational institutions to pivot towards STEM, digital fluency, and problem-solving skills.[2]

Japan, in a bid to transform into "Society 5.0," an AI-driven utopia, is overhauling its education blueprint. With the launch of the GIGA School Program, Japanese schools are experiencing a digital makeover, fostering an environment conducive to innovative pedagogical practices.[3]

Meanwhile, South Korea is placing its chips on the AI bet with substantial investments. Plans are in motion to create six AI-focused graduate schools, while a remarkable 2.2 trillion won is earmarked for AI research over five years, an ambitious step toward the vision of South Korea as a global AI power by 2030.[4]

China's New Generation Artificial Intelligence Development Plan echoes the same goal but with a twist – China seeks to ascend the throne as the world's AI overlord by 2030. Universities across the Middle Kingdom are expanding their AI curricula and research; institutions like Peking University are even launching AI-exclusive schools.[5,6]

The island nation of Singapore is no straggler either. TechSkills Accelerator Initiative, a collaborative venture of the Infocomm Media Development Authority (IMDA) and SkillsFuture Singapore (SSG), offers a suite of AI foundational courses.[7] The National University of Singapore (NUS) has also taken a leap into the AI arena with an AI specialization under its Bachelor of Technology program.[8]

Yet, all these progressions cast long shadows of challenges. These range from keeping pace with the speed-of-light evolution of technology, ensuring democratic access to digital tools, and training educators to become tech-savvy. A glaring example surfaces in Australia, where a 2019 survey by the National Centre for Vocational Education Research found that a mere 49 percent of vocational teachers felt at ease wielding digital technology in their classrooms.[9]

In sum, the advent of technological disruptions calls for universities, governments, and policymakers to transition from passive observers to active players. By aligning higher education with the reality of an AI-dominated world, they can equip students to thrive, not just survive, in the digitized future.

Online Learning and the Abyss of Digital Inequity

The rapid advancement in technology, particularly in the realms of augmented reality and virtual reality, is reshaping the landscape of higher education. As these technologies become more accessible, they are opening up new avenues for immersive and interactive learning experiences, far beyond traditional classroom settings. This transition is not just driven by necessity but also by the progressive integration of these innovations into everyday life. Alongside, there's a growing recognition of the importance of environmental sustainability in education. Institutions are increasingly adopting green technologies and sustainable practices, both in physical infrastructure and in digital learning environments. However, these advancements also bring to light the issue of equitable access. The challenge now lies in ensuring that these innovative educational tools are not just available to a select few but are accessible to students across various socioeconomic backgrounds, thereby bridging the technology accessibility gap. As universities scramble to adjust, digital learning, underpinned by bleeding-edge technology, is fast becoming the cornerstone of education in this decade. But in its wake, it has laid bare an unsettling and persistent truth – the deep-rooted digital divide.

One evolving aspect is the role of artificial intelligence in education. As outlined by the Brookings Institution, there's an emerging concept of a new digital divide related to AI. This divide is not just about having access to technology but also about having access to the necessary skills and support to effectively utilize AI in educational settings. This new divide presents a challenge. While AI offers the promise of personalized learning and can help bridge gaps where there are shortages of qualified teachers, it also requires a set of skills and supports that may not be equally accessible to all students.

The 2023 Digital Education Outlook by the OECD delves into the state of digital education transformation. It emphasizes the critical need for robust internet connectivity and educational tools like student information systems and learning-management systems. However, the report notes a gap in how these tools are being leveraged to provide real-time information and comprehensive assessment data. Furthermore, there is a significant emphasis on the evolving role of educators in the digital era. The preparedness of educators to navigate digital changes and their ability to access digital resources is crucial. The report highlights a gap in educator preparedness and the need for extensive training at all service stages.[10]

These insights suggest that the digital divide in education is becoming more complex. It's not just about having devices and internet access; it's increasingly about how effectively these technologies are integrated into the education system, how well educators and students are prepared to use them, and how equitably these resources are distributed.

To address this, there's a need for a holistic approach that encompasses policy frameworks, infrastructure development, and a culture that supports continuous adaptation and learning. Such an approach should aim not only to provide the hardware of digital education but also to ensure that educators and students have the skills and support necessary to make the most of these digital tools. This comprehensive strategy can help turn the digital transition into a meaningful transformation that benefits all students equitably.

In the Asia-Pacific theater, the panorama of digital disparity isn't any rosier. The Asia Cloud Computing Association's 2020 survey reveals the existence of a digital divide in every country surveyed, including tech juggernauts like Australia, Japan, South Korea, China, Taiwan, and Singapore. In China, approximately 37 percent of students were forced to resort to mobile phones for online learning due to an acute shortage of suitable devices.[11]

South Korea and Singapore, despite their reputations as technology powerhouses, haven't been spared from the digital divide. In South Korea, marginalized groups, including low-income households and the elderly, find themselves on the wrong side of the digital divide, even amid an impressive 97.57 percent internet penetration rate in 2021.[12] Similarly, in Singapore, an estimated 28,000 households were stranded without internet access in 2022.[13,14]

Countries beyond the Asia-Pacific, like Saudi Arabia and nations on the African continent, grapple with their bespoke versions of the digital divide. Saudi Arabia, despite making strides under the aegis of the Saudi Vision 2030 project, designed to supercharge the digital economy, is wrestling with the challenge of equitable online education delivery, particularly for students tucked away in remote regions.[15]

The situation in Africa is particularly concerning, largely attributable to the digital divide enveloping the continent. As per data from the International Telecommunication Union, only a mere 28 percent of Africa's populace had access to the internet in 2019, a stark digital desertification that hampers the transition towards online education.[16]

Bridging the digital divide warrants a united front from universities, governments, and policymakers. Potential antidotes include substantial investments in digital infrastructure, particularly in technologically neglected regions, subsidized or free internet access for students, and policies that make digital tools more pocket friendly.

Singapore's "DigitalAccess@Home" Programme[17] and South Korea's "Public Wi-Fi Project"[18] are testaments to the progress that can be achieved. The former reaches out to students and people with disabilities from low-income households, offering them affordable computers and internet connectivity. The latter aims to democratize internet access by providing free Wi-Fi in public zones nationwide.

While online learning dangles the prospect of a more inclusive higher education ecosystem, it's a promise that rings hollow unless we grapple with the specter of digital inequity. For the transition to online learning to realize its full potential, it needs to serve as a catalyst for equality, not a perpetuator of the digital divide.

The Interplay of Demographics and Internationalization

With the ongoing trend of globalization, universities are increasingly becoming diverse hubs, welcoming a growing number of international students. This shift has transformed many institutions into centers of varied cultural representation, reflecting a broader global perspective in the student body. The transnational student migration trend has been on a steady ascent. The UNESCO Institute for Statistics (2021) indicates an upward trend in the count of globe-trotting students, rising from 5.4 million registered in 2017 to 6.4 million in 2021.[19]

Institutions are also reworking their financial models and revenue streams to achieve sustainability, a trend that reflects the need to diversify income sources and reduce overreliance on specific student demographics, such as international students. Inclusion and support services are being strengthened to build connections, acceptance, and success among students, emphasizing the importance of a diverse and inclusive campus culture.

Moreover, increased marketing spending is putting pressure on universities to demonstrate quantifiable results, indicating a shift toward data-driven strategies in attracting and retaining students. These trends suggest that institutions are adapting to changing demographics and globalization pressures by embracing alternative strategies and evolving their operations to remain competitive and relevant in the educational landscape.

These developments highlight a strategic and future-forward approach to higher education, focusing not just on traditional academic offerings but also on the broader experience and support systems that cater to an increasingly diverse and global student population.

As we reflect on the outcomes of Japan's Global 30 initiative, launched with the aim of attracting 300,000 international students by 2020, it's clear that the project's ambitions have met with mixed results.[20] While universities expanded their English-taught programs and bolstered support for international students, Japan's demographic challenges, including declining birth rates and an aging population, have influenced the dynamics of its academic environment. The current focus is now on assessing the impact of these efforts and adapting strategies to align with the evolving global and domestic educational landscape.

South Korea is another player in the international student recruitment game. With a robust international student community of over 160,000 in 2019, the South Korean government's Study Korea 2020 Project aims to stoke these numbers further, setting a target of 200,000 by the end of 2023.[21] However, they'll have to address simmering issues of social integration and student support to truly realize this vision.

China, the giant in the East, has emerged as a major contender on the global education stage. With impressive inbound and outbound student traffic, China housed more than 492,185 international students as of 2018, according to the Ministry of Education.[22] With the advent of the Double First Class initiative, aimed at boosting domestic universities' global standing, the floodgates for international students could swing open even wider. The Double First Class initiative in China, initiated in 2015, is a significant strategic step aimed at enhancing the nation's higher education system. It focuses on developing world-class universities and top-tier academic disciplines to bolster China's educational standing globally. The initiative's first phase, which concluded in 2020, involved reforms in talent training, research management, and performance evaluation.[23]

As of 2022, the initiative entered its second phase, expanding its list to include 147 universities and 331 disciplines. This expansion reflects China's ongoing commitment to elevating its educational institutions to a global standard. Notably, top-ranked institutions like Peking University and Tsinghua University have been granted autonomy to evaluate and confirm which of their own disciplines qualify for the project. This autonomy is a new development in the project's second phase.[24]

The initiative aims to make China a "powerful country of education" by 2035, with a long-term focus on nurturing top talent and meeting strategic national demands. However, it also raises concerns about widening the gap between selected and non-selected universities and disciplines in terms of funding, reputation, and student admissions, potentially leading to a more pronounced hierarchical structure in China's higher education system.[23]

Singapore, a buzzing cosmopolitan city-state, has carved out a niche as an education powerhouse in Asia, magnetizing students from the region and beyond. While the allure of a high-quality education and multicultural milieu is hard to resist, issues of student integration and steep living costs stand as roadblocks.

Europe, with the Erasmus+ program, has been a shining beacon of student mobility within its borders. However, the uncertainties of Brexit loom large over the UK's participation in the program, casting a cloud over the international student flux.[25]

Africa, often overlooked, is increasingly recognized as an untapped reservoir for international students, especially for students within the continent. Countries such as Morocco, South Africa, and Rwanda are experiencing a surge in regional student movement. However, they'll have to grapple with infrastructural constraints, the quality of education, and language barriers.[26]

In the Middle East, Saudi Arabia's Vision 2030 strategy carves out a role for international students in the country's bid to diversify its oil-dependent economy.[15] However, they'll have to navigate the murky waters of academic freedom and women's rights to draw a broad spectrum of students.

In light of these trends, universities across the globe will have to perform a delicate balancing act, adjusting their curricula, campus culture, and support systems to cater to an increasingly diverse and international student body. Governments, too, will need to tailor immigration and education policies that ease international student mobility and ensure inclusivity. If handled deftly, universities can continue to serve as global nerve centers of knowledge, innovation, and cultural exchange, at the forefront of the new world order.

Universities and the Pandemic's Fiscal Fallout

The COVID-19 pandemic has gripped the globe, throttling economies and leaving in its wake a trail of fiscal desolation that has found its way into universities worldwide. This financial instability has sent ripples of apprehension through the higher-education sector, leaving universities staring down a financial abyss as they wrestle with shrinking revenues and burgeoning costs.

The United States, often a bellwether in global trends, has been hit hard. The American Council on Education estimated, before a December relief package, that colleges and universities needed $120 billion to offset pandemic-induced financial challenges.[27] This financial hemorrhage could cripple the quality of education, impair research capabilities, and strip crucial financial aid from the hands of students. American universities, traditionally reliant on tuition and endowment funds, face financial strain due to declining enrollment and decreased international student numbers. Strategies could include increasing online program offerings and seeking alternative revenue sources like corporate partnerships and continuing-education programs.

The fiscal gloom has cast a shadow far beyond US shores. Australian universities, traditionally buoyed by international students' fees, have found their coffers significantly depleted in the face of stalled international travel. Universities Australia's grim forecast estimates that the higher-education sector stands to lose a considerable AU$16 billion from 2020 to 2023, due to the plummet in international student enrollment.[28]

In Japan, public universities have found some solace in substantial government funding. But their private counterparts, accounting for a hefty 80 percent of all universities, found themselves teetering on the edge of financial viability even before the pandemic struck. The situation is further compounded by a rapidly aging population and a decreasing number of college-age students, leading to increasingly tighter financial constraints.[29,30] Post-"Global 30," Japan's universities may need to diversify their international student recruitment strategies and strengthen alumni networks globally. Additionally, focusing on collaborative research programs with international institutions can enhance their global appeal.

Private universities in South Korea echo a similar sentiment. The government's subsidies for 192 private universities increased every year, and it amounted to approximately 3.18 trillion South Korean won in 2021, a financial quagmire that the pandemic is likely to have deepened.[31] South Korean universities might focus on enhancing their technological infrastructure to support innovative research and attract global talent. Partnerships with tech industries and increased emphasis on STEM fields could provide new growth avenues.

China, where higher education largely leans on government funding, has not escaped unscathed. The economic fallout of the pandemic, compounded by a strategic shift toward bankrolling top-tier universities to bolster global rankings, may leave lower-tier institutions stranded financially. The shift toward funding elite universities in China to improve global rankings could exacerbate inequalities within the higher education system.[32] One strategy to mitigate this could be increasing investment in vocational and technical education, which can provide diverse educational pathways and support regional development. This approach may also help in addressing skills gaps in the Chinese economy.

Singaporean universities, predominantly state funded, have managed to stay afloat better than many. However, the long shadow of economic downturn raises concerns about the sustainability of funding in the long run. While Singaporean universities have managed well, diversifying funding sources could be key to future sustainability. This might include fostering stronger industry partnerships, encouraging private investment, and developing more robust alumni networks. Such measures can provide alternative revenue streams and reduce dependency on state funding.

In Europe, the fiscal landscape is a patchwork of varied scenarios. UK universities, already grappling with the uncertainties of Brexit, now face a double whammy as the pandemic disrupts the inflow of international students – a crucial revenue lifeline. In contrast, German universities, largely state funded, have demonstrated resilience, but concerns simmer about the pandemic's longer-term impacts. UK universities facing challenges from Brexit and pandemic impacts could explore expanding their online- and distance-learning programs to reach a global student base. Additionally, forging international partnerships for research and student-exchange programs might help mitigate the loss of EU funding and collaborations.

Despite their resilience, German universities should prepare for potential financial challenges. Emphasizing interdisciplinary research and innovation can attract more international funding and partnerships. Moreover, enhancing collaboration between universities and industries can open new funding avenues and ensure the practical relevance of academic programs.

Africa's universities, perennially underfunded, are caught in a double bind, with the necessary pivot to online learning placing unprecedented strain on already thin resources. With many African nations battling economic obstacles, the education budget could be thrust further into the crosshairs. African universities, grappling with underfunding and the shift to online learning, might benefit from international partnerships and grants. Collaborations with global universities can provide both financial support and access to digital resources. Additionally, fostering local private-sector partnerships could provide both funding and relevant training opportunities for students.

In the Middle East, Saudi Arabian universities, heavily reliant on government largesse, could find their budgets slashed in response to plummeting oil prices. With potential budget cuts, Saudi universities could focus on developing endowment funds and seeking alternative funding sources like private investments. Expanding collaboration with international universities and investing in emerging fields like renewable energy can also provide new opportunities for funding and research.

In the face of these formidable financial headwinds, universities globally will have to chart a new course. Strategies could encompass fostering public-private partnerships, tapping into the generosity of alumni, monetizing online course offerings, and exploring innovative financing mechanisms such as income-share agreements (ISAs). Policymakers will have to take a hard look at budget allocations, finding ways to shore up or stabilize funding for higher education to ensure its sustainability in a post-pandemic world.

Mental Health Crisis in Universities

University campuses around the globe are facing an escalating mental health challenge, a situation further intensified by the COVID-19 pandemic. As students grapple with the stresses of pandemic-induced isolation, a cloud of uncertainty about the future, and academic pressures, the number of mental health issues on campuses is alarmingly on the rise.

In the United States, the situation is reaching a tipping point. A survey from a sample exceeding 350,000 students across 373 campuses, conducted by a Boston University researcher in early 2021, indicates more than 60 percent of students met the criteria for one or more mental health problems, reflecting an almost 50 percent increase compared to 2013, reaching its highest levels due to various stress factors like the coronavirus pandemic and political unrest.[33]

In Australia, a survey conducted by Headspace (2020) unveils a worrying reality. Australian young people (aged twelve to twenty-five) are under the gun, with an astonishing one in three young people reporting high or very high levels of psychological distress, a testament to the stressors they face.[34]

In Japan, a study in *Psychiatry and Clinical Neurosciences* (2021) revealed that the suicide rate (20 percent) per 100,000 undergraduate students in 2020–21 was the highest compared to the previous six academic years, highlighting the profound mental health challenges confronting students.[35]

South Korean universities are in the throes of a mental health crisis of their own. The Korean Educational Development Institute's troubling revelation is that 39.6 percent of students experienced depressive symptoms in 2019.[36] This unsettling reality spurred the implementation of mental health classes in a host of universities.

In China, a nation of over a billion people, mental health struggles among students are widespread. A study showcased in the *European Child & Adolescent Psychiatry* (2020) highlighted that 43.7 percent of Chinese students were having depressive symptoms.[37]

In Taiwan, the escalating mental health crisis is evident. The Ministry of Education (2020) reported a steady uptick in the number of students seeking mental health services over the past half-decade.[38]

In Saudi Arabia, a study featured in the *Journal of American College Health* (2021) found that over 48.8 percent of university students displayed symptoms of mental health disorders, with anxiety and depression being particularly rampant.[39]

The situation in Africa is even graver, with mental health services at universities drastically underfunded and under-resourced. A study published in *BMC Psychiatry* (2019) disclosed that 30 percent of university students in Ethiopia displayed symptoms of depression, anxiety, or stress.[40]

In Europe, the mental health crisis among students is equally concerning. A 2022 study in *Current Biology* unveiled a substantial rise in psychological distress in 2020.[41]

In Singapore, the National University of Singapore's survey (2019) found that one in four students reported battling mental health issues, underscoring the pervasiveness of the problem.[42]

Faced with this ticking mental health time bomb, universities must rally their resources to invest in mental health services, cultivate a supportive and understanding culture, and empower faculty and staff with the tools to recognize and respond to mental health issues. They must also facilitate open and honest dialogues about mental health, to chip away at the stigma associated with it and encourage students to reach out when help is needed. Partnering with external mental health providers could also broaden the reach and improve the quality of support available for students. Policymakers must also enter the fray, formulating policies that ensure the provision and accessibility of mental health support in educational institutions.

Turning Crisis into Opportunity

As a swarm of challenges descends upon universities worldwide, it will take a united front from all stakeholders to meet them head-on. Universities will need to transform into agile institutions, continually reshaping their curricula, teaching methods, and support systems to cater to evolving needs.

Take Australian universities, for example. Already ahead of the curve, pioneering institutions such as Monash University, has instituted tech-forward courses and majors in response to the burgeoning demand for digital skills.[43] These programs are designed to meet the increasing demand for digital skills, positioning students for success in a tech-driven world. This approach reflects the universities' commitment to staying ahead of the curve in providing relevant and future-focused education.

Meanwhile, in South Korea, the government has thrown its weight behind online learning platforms like K-MOOC to navigate the swift currents toward digital education and help close the digital divide.[44] Universities are starting to adopt a more holistic approach, assessing applicants based on their backgrounds, personal narratives, and extracurricular activities, alongside their academic performance. This shift aims to engender a diverse student body and nurture a more inclusive campus culture.

In Saudi Arabia, the government has taken the initiative to foster partnerships with private enterprises to fund research and innovation at universities.[45] This strategy aims to diversify their income in the face of looming financial challenges.

African universities are taking a digital-first approach to connect with students in remote areas.[46] Simultaneously, in Europe, attention is turning to promoting students' mental well-being. Initiatives like the European University Foundation's Healthy Campus project exemplify this focus.[47]

In Singapore, universities like the National University of Singapore are placing significant emphasis on lifelong learning, rolling out mini-courses and skills-based training modules to keep pace with the ever-shifting job market.[48]

Beyond the universities, policymakers have an instrumental role to play by providing legislative backing and crucial financial support and keeping education high on their agenda.[49] An example of this is the Japanese government's "Super Global Universities" funding initiative, which supports university endeavors to globalize their campuses and curricula.[50]

Students, families, and university staff should keep abreast of these trends, girding themselves for a potentially turbulent era. Creating opportunities amid these challenges will call for a spirit of collaboration and innovation. Universities and industries can form alliances to ensure the relevance of education. Policymakers can bring students and educators into the fold when making decisions, fostering a more democratic and responsive education system.

If stakeholders can work in concert, they can transform these challenges into opportunities, sculpting a resilient, inclusive, and effective higher-education sector fit for the future. As universities across the globe grapple with these issues, global collaboration in higher education will be critical. They can glean valuable insights from each other's successes and failures in tackling these challenges. The race is on to shape the universities of tomorrow.

References

1 J. Manyika, S. Lund, M. Chui, J. Bughin, J. Woetzel, P. Batra, and S. Sanghvi (2017). "Jobs Lost, Jobs Gained: What the Future of Work Will Mean for Jobs, Skills, And Wages," *McKinsey Global Institute Series*, 150(1), 1–148.
2 Commonwealth of Australia (2015). "National Innovation and Science Agenda Report," accessed October 10, 2023, https://www.industry.gov.au/publications/national-innovation-and-science-agenda-report.
3 "Japan Pushing Ahead with Society 5.0 to Overcome Chronic Social Challenges," accessed October 10, 2023, https://www.unesco.org/en/articles/japan-pushing-ahead-society-50-overcome-chronic-social-challenges.
4 "South Korea to Invest 2.2 Trillion Won in Bid to Seize the Lead in AI Technology by 2022," accessed October 10, 2023, https://opengovasia.com/south-korea-to-invest-2-2-trillion-won-in-bid-to-seize-the-lead-in-ai-technology-by-2022/.
5 "Full Translation: China's 'New Generation Artificial Intelligence Development Plan'" (2017), accessed October 10, 2023, https://www.newamerica.org/cybersecurity-initiative/digichina/blog/full-translation-chinas-new-generation-artificial-intelligence-development-plan-2017/.
6 F. Wu, Q. He, and C. Wu (2021). "AI+ X Micro-Program Fosters Interdisciplinary Skills in China," *Communications of the ACM*, 64(11), 52–54.
7 "TechSkills Accelerator (TeSA)," accessed October 10, 2023, https://www.imda.gov.sg/how-we-can-help/techskills-accelerator-tesa.
8 "NUS-ISS: Artificial Intelligence," accessed October 10, 2023, https://www.iss.nus.edu.sg/executive-education/discipline/detail/artificial-intelligence.
9 V. Gekara, D. Snell, A. Molla, S. Karanasios, and A. Thomas (2019). "Skilling the Australian Workforce for the Digital Economy," *Research Report, National Centre for Vocational Education Research (NCVER)*, accessed October 10, 2023, https://www.ncver.edu.au/__data/assets/pdf_file/0026/5744123/Skilling-the-Australian-workforce-for-the-digital-economy.pdf.

10 "Some U.S. students Lack Home Internet or Computer for Homework," *Pew Research Center*, accessed October 10, 2023, https://www.pewresearch.org/fact-tank/2018/10/26/nearly-one-in-five-teens-cant-always-finish-their-homework-because-of-the-digital-divide.
11 C. Guo, Z. Xu, C. Fang, and B. Qin (2022). "China Survey Report on the Online Learning Status of High Schools During the COVID-19 Pandemic," *ECNU Review of Education*, 1, 1–13, https://doi.org/10.1177/20965311221089671.
12 "Percentage of Population Using the Internet in South Korea from 2000 to 2021," *Statista*, accessed October 10, 2023, https://www.statista.com/statistics/255859/internet-penetration-in-south-korea/.
13 "New Scheme to Help 60,000 Lower-Income Families Obtain Internet Access, Digital Devices," *Channel News Asia*, accessed October 10, 2023, https://www.channelnewsasia.com/singapore/digital-access-inclusivity-internet-broadband-lower-income-households-3311231.
14 "Number of Households in Singapore from 2013 to 2022," *Statista*, accessed October 10, 2023, https://www.statista.com/statistics/728350/number-of-households-singapore/.
15 "Saudi Vision 2030," accessed October 10, 2023, https://www.vision2030.gov.sa/.
16 "Online Education Market in Africa," *Digitaldefynd*, accessed October 10, 2023, https://digitaldefynd.com/IQ/online-education-market-africa/.
17 "DigitalAccess@Home," *Infocomm Media Development Authority*, accessed October 10, 2023, https://www.imda.gov.sg/how-we-can-help/digital-access-at-home.
18 "KT to Expand South Korea's Free Public Wi-Fi Availability," *ZDNet*, accessed October 10, 2023, https://www.zdnet.com/home-and-office/networking/kt-to-expand-south-koreas-free-public-wi-fi-availability/.
19 "Inbound/Outbound Internationally Mobile Students by Host Region," *UNESO Institute for Statistics*, accessed October 10, 2023, http://data.uis.unesco.org/.
20 C. Burgess, I. Gibson, J. Klaphake, and M. Selzer (2010). "The 'Global 30' Project and Japanese Higher Education Reform: An Example of a 'Closing in' or an 'Opening up'?" *Globalisation, Societies and Education*, 8(4), 461–475.
21 E. Choi (2022). "The Korean Case of International Student Recruitment: Remarkable Progress but Internally Flawed," in *International Student Recruitment and Mobility In Non-Anglophone Countries* (pp. 216–234), Routledge.
22 "2018 Statistical Report on International Students in China," *Ministry of Education of the People's Republic of China*, accessed October 10, 2023, http://en.moe.gov.cn/news/media_highlights/201904/t20190415_377952.html.
23 S. Liu, X. Luo, and M. Liu (2023). "Was Chinese 'Double-First Class' Construction Policy Influential? Analysis Using Propensity Score Matching," *Sustainability*, 15(8), 6378.
24 "China Expands Double First Class Universities List," *The Times Higher Education*, accessed December 16, 2023, https://www.timeshighereducation.com/news/china-expands-double-first-class-universities-list.
25 "The UK and Erasmus+," *Erasmus+*, accessed December 16, 2023, https://erasmus-plus.ec.europa.eu/the-uk-and-erasmus.
26 "Intraregional Student Mobility in Sub-Saharan Africa. World Education," *News & Reviews (WENR)*, accessed December 30, https://wenr.wes.org/2023/10/intraregional-student-mobility-in-sub-saharan-africa.
27 "Statement by Ace President Ted Mitchell on COVID-19 Relief Package Higher Education Funding," *American Council on Education*, accessed October 10, 2023, https://www.acenet.edu/News-Room/Pages/Statement-by-ACE-President-Ted-Mitchell-on-COVID-19-Relief-Package-Higher-Education-Funding.aspx.

28 "COVID-19 to Cost Universities $16 Billion by 2023," *Universities Australia*, accessed October 10, 2023, https://universitiesaustralia.edu.au/media-item/covid-19-to-cost-universities-16-billion-by-2023/.
29 J. Breaden and R. Goodman (2023). "Reforms in Japan's Private Universities," *International Higher Education*, 113, 34–35.
30 "Japanese Universities Losing Battle with Foreign Rivals," *Deutsche Welle*, accessed December 16, 2023, https://www.dw.com/en/japanese-universities-losing-battle-with-foreign-rivals/a-66505357.
31 "Government Subsidies for Private Universities in South Korea In 2021, by Type of Financial Support (in Billion South Korean Won)," *Statista*, accessed October 10, 2023, https://www.statista.com/statistics/1240541/south-korea-government-subsidies-for-private-universities-by-type-of-financial-support.
32 L. Xu, C. Xie, and J. Lei (2021). "Discursive Marketisation through Positive Evaluation: A Diachronic Analysis of About us Texts of Top-Tier Chinese Universities over the Past Two Decades," *Frontiers in Psychology*, 12, 789558.
33 S. K. Lipson, S. Zhou, S. Abelson, J. Heinze, M. Jirsa, J. Morigney, and D. Eisenberg (2022). "Trends in College Student Mental Health and Help-Seeking by Race/Ethnicity: Findings from the National Healthy Minds Study, 2013–2021," *Journal of Affective Disorders*, 306, 138–147.
34 "Insights: Youth Mental Health and Wellbeing Over Time—Headspace National Youth Mental Health Survey 2020," *Headspace*, accessed October 10, 2023, https://headspace.org.au/assets/Uploads/Insights-youth-mental-health-and-wellbeing-over-time-headspace-National-Youth-Mental-Health-Survey-2020.pdf.
35 Y. Fuse-Nagase, T. Marutani, H. Tachikawa, T. Iwami, Y. Yamamoto, T. Moriyama, and K. Yasumi (2021). "Increase in Suicide Rates Among Undergraduate Students in Japanese National Universities During the COVID-19 Pandemic," *Psychiatry and Clinical Neurosciences*, 75(11), 351.
36 J. Lee, Y.-H. Ko, S. Chi, M.-S. Lee, and H.-K. Yoon (2022). "Impact of the COVID-19 Pandemic on Korean Adolescents' Mental Health And Lifestyle Factors," *Journal of Adolescent Health*, 71(3), 270–276.
37 S. J. Zhou, L. G. Zhang, L. L. Wang, Z. C. Guo, J. Q. Wang, J. C. Chen, and J. X. Chen (2020). "Prevalence and Socio-Demographic Correlates of Psychological Health Problems in Chinese Adolescents During the Outbreak of COVID-19," *European Child & Adolescent Psychiatry*, 29, 749–758.
38 "More Schools Let Students Take Mental Health Leave," *Taipei Times*, accessed December 30, https://www.taipeitimes.com/News/taiwan/archives/2023/09/25/2003806752.
39 N. AlHadi and A. M. Alhuwaydi (2021). "The Mental Health Impact of Pandemic COVID-19 Crisis on University Students in Saudi Arabia and Associated Factors," *Journal of American College Health*, 71(6), 1854–1862.
40 G. Ahmed, A. Negash, H. Kerebih, D. Alemu, and Y. Tesfaye (2020). "Prevalence and Associated Factors of Depression among Jimma University Students. A Cross-Sectional Study," *International Journal of Mental Health System*s, 14, 1–10.
41 "Building Resilience Is Key to Good Mental Health: NUS Youth Epidemiology and Resilience Study," *National University of Singapore*, https://medicine.nus.edu.sg/wp-content/uploads/2023/04/PRESS-RELEASE-YEAR-Study-26APR2023-IMMEDIATE-RELEASE.pdf.
42 R. Allen, C. Kannangara, M. Vyas, and J. Carson (2022). "European University Students' Mental Health during COVID-19: Exploring Attitudes towards COVID-19 and Governmental Response," *Current Psychology*, 42, 20165–20178.
43 "Future Skills," *Monash University*, accessed December 30, https://www.monash.edu/monash-professional-pathways/digital-skills.

44 "Korean Massive Open Online Course (K-MOOC)," accessed October 10, 2023, http://www.kmooc.kr/.
45 "Saudi Looks to Global Partnerships to Fuel Research, Development and Innovation," *Oxford Business Group*, accessed December 30, https://oxfordbusinessgroup.com/reports/saudi-arabia/2023-report/innovation/global-collaboration-efforts-are-under-way-to-diversify-international-partnerships-and-fuel-research-development-and-innovation-analysis.
46 "The Response of Higher Education to COVID-19-Higher Education in Africa: Challenges and Solutions through ICT, Online Training, Distance Education and Digital Inclusion," *UNESCO*, accessed December 30, https://www.unesco.org/en/articles/response-higher-education-covid-19-higher-education-africa-challenges-and-solutions-through-ict.
47 "European University Foundation," accessed December 30, https://uni-foundation.eu/.
48 "NUS Lifelong Learning (L³)," *National University of Singapore*, accessed December 30, https://scale.nus.edu.sg/programmes/lifelonglearning.
49 "How Policymakers Can Help Higher Education Better Serve Students," *The Education Trust*, accessed December 30, https://edtrust.org/the-equity-line/how-policymakers-can-help-higher-education-better-serve-students/.
50 "Top Global University Project," *Ministry of Education, Culture, Sports, Science and Technology – Japan*, accessed December 30, https://tgu.mext.go.jp/en/index.html.

11 Intriguing Prelude

The Tech-Dominant Future

As we hurtle into the future, one can't help but anticipate an academic landscape nearly unrecognizable from today's. Picture this – five years hence, AI-powered chatbots could become the new digital gatekeepers, presiding over everything from admissions to student services, a metamorphosis prompted by the likes of Georgia State University's AI advising system.[1] Ten years on, we may witness AI and machine learning penetrating the sanctum of teaching, crafting individualized tutoring experiences that harmonize with each learner's pace and style. Fast forward fifteen years, we might find ourselves in an epoch where AI systems not only grade assignments across myriad subjects but also provide critical feedback. Simultaneously, data analytics might predict student performance and dropout risk with uncanny precision, preempting the need for early interventions. The rise of virtual and augmented reality could further blur the lines between physical and digital, culminating in a transformation of higher education that we're only beginning to grasp.

Shattering Silos: The Rise of Interdisciplinary Learning

Imagine an academic future unshackled from the constraints of traditional disciplines. Five years from now, universities may birth a new generation of interdisciplinary programs, similar to bioinformatics, designed to tackle the complex challenges of our era. A decade down the line, students could be the architects of their educational journey, curating degrees around specific skills and knowledge areas. In this future, traditional classroom learning may be replaced by project-based formats that weave together diverse disciplines. Move fifteen years into the future, and the lines between disciplines might blur completely, with universities, industries, and governments collaborating to offer immersive, experiential learning. In this world, education could shift from mere knowledge acquisition to innovative application, reinforcing the power of interdisciplinary learning in a rapidly evolving world.

DOI: 10.4324/9781003476504-12

The Ethics Evolution: Humanizing the Future of Tech

In the near future, universities may transform into epicenters of a crucial dialogue: the interplay of ethics and technology. In five years, the academic landscape may be populated with programs that mirror the University of Oxford's pioneering "Ethics of AI,"[2] merging technological mastery with a discerning ethical lens. Jump ahead another five years, and the significance of ethics in technology education may reach a crescendo. Ethics, no longer a mere footnote, could inhabit the heart of curricula across tech disciplines, fueled by real-world case studies and robust industry alliances. Advance to fifteen years hence, and we may witness a world where ethicists stand shoulder to shoulder with technologists in academia. In this envisioned future, an ethics module may become a nonnegotiable part of any degree involving data or technology, rooting tomorrow's tech leaders in a bedrock of ethical understanding. Amid this shift, universities could prioritize research focused on curtailing technology's societal fallout, underscoring their dual roles as knowledge creators and societal sentinels.

Riding the Wave of Transformation: The Lifelong Learning Odyssey and the Reshaping of Skill Development

Within a five-year horizon, we'll witness a transformation in higher education, driven by the growing necessity for continuous learning and skill enhancement. Expect to see universities expanding their offerings with a range of online courses, short-term certifications, and professional development programs. This expansion will likely include collaborations with platforms like edX and Coursera. A decade from now, the traditional four-year degree model might evolve into a more flexible, modular format. Here, students can accumulate stackable credentials over time, eventually forming a complete degree. AI technology could become central in this scenario, tailoring educational paths to each individual's interests, career aspirations, and learning preferences. Looking fifteen years ahead, the lines between academic study and professional life may blur, as lifelong learning becomes integral to career progression. Universities could become ongoing centers of learning, providing consistent support throughout a person's career in a technology-driven world.

Sustainability as the Guiding Star: A Glimpse into the University of the Future

Within the next half-decade, expect universities to become key players in the sustainability revolution, integrating environmental consciousness into all aspects of their teaching and operations. Courses will likely blend sustainability into various disciplines, and new programs focused on global ecological challenges may arise. Moving ahead another decade, universities might position themselves at the forefront of sustainable innovation, establishing dedicated research centers to address critical global issues. Their academic focus could shift toward a problem-solving model that includes digital and environmental sustainability. In fifteen years, sustainability could be central to university operations, with institutions potentially achieving carbon neutrality and zero waste, and playing a pivotal role in shaping a sustainable future in collaboration with government and industry. Concurrently, universities will need to navigate the digital transformation of education, balancing the ecological impacts and societal benefits of digital technologies.

Education Unbound: The Evolution of Academic Disciplines in a Technological Age

In five years, universities are likely to witness the rise of disciplines such as data science, machine learning, and cybersecurity, propelled by AI and automation advancements. Quantum computing and nanotechnology may establish stronger footholds in academia, with interdisciplinary studies exploring the societal and ethical implications of digital technology gaining popularity. A decade later, these nascent fields could be well-established, joined by emerging areas like genetic engineering and space exploration. Fifteen years from now, the academic world might showcase a dynamic mix of interdisciplinary areas, moving away from traditional departmental structures. Cutting-edge fields like advanced bioinformatics and neurotechnology could become prominent, reflecting a world increasingly focused on the intersections of technology, social science, and ethics, with universities evolving into centers of lifelong learning.

Reimagining Physical Infrastructure: The Physical-to-Digital Metamorphosis

As we step into the future, universities may find their physical foundations reinvented within the next five years, potentially pivoting from large campuses to decentralized models, courtesy of digital and remote learning advancements. A decade ahead, university campuses could undergo a significant redesign to accommodate hybrid education models that blend physical and digital domains. The arrival of technologies like 6G, personalized AI, and AI and Machine Learning–assisted IoT might foster "smart campuses" – connected, interactive, and adaptable spaces for versatile educational needs.

Fifteen years hence, we might witness a reframing of the idea of a physical campus. Smaller, multifunctional spaces facilitating collaborative and individual learning could become the norm. Universities may create "university districts," blending academia, industry, and local communities. The concept of virtual campuses could gain prominence, utilizing advanced VR and AR technologies to create immersive digital learning experiences.

In essence, the future physical infrastructure of universities might be a harmonious fusion of tradition and innovation, a fluid educational ecosystem where the physical enables and extends digital reach. These transformative spaces will reflect the university's evolution, aligning with the diverse needs of future learners and the changing landscape of academia.

Revolutionizing the Academic Endeavor: The Future of Research in a Technologically Advanced Age

In the near future, technology will profoundly transform the research landscape at universities. Over the next five years, machine learning algorithms may become integral to data analysis, while quantum computing could start to accelerate scientific discovery across fields from sociology to environmental science. Fast forward a decade, and universities could be leading the integration of AI, quantum computing, and emerging technologies like genetic engineering in their research. They may also adopt open-science practices, leading to a global, collaborative, and transparent research ecosystem.

Fifteen years from now, the research landscape may be unrecognizable. Universities could become nodes in global research networks, leveraging AI and virtual reality to facilitate intense, interdisciplinary collaboration. They would also harness AI-driven data analytics to parse vast data troves, making predictions in diverse fields like climate change and human behavior. Technology will also form part of the research subject matter, with fields like digital humanities and computational social science gaining prominence. Concurrently, universities could prioritize ethical research into societal impacts and moral implications of advanced technologies.

In sum, technology will enable universities to transcend traditional research boundaries, empowering them to probe more profound questions, collaborate more effectively, and share their findings more widely. As research becomes more global, interdisciplinary, and inclusive, universities will remain pivotal in driving knowledge and discovery.

Universities as Vanguard of Climate Action: Education, Research, and Sustainability Practices

In the next five years, universities may prioritize climate literacy across disciplines. Specialized degrees in climate science, renewable energy, and sustainability studies could emerge, aligning education with the realities of a world impacted by climate change.

Fastforward a decade, and universities may refocus their research toward sustainability goals. Interdisciplinary research hubs could rise, driving solutions for climate change by merging environmental science, technology, social science, and policy-making.

Fifteen years into the future, universities might become paragons of sustainable practices. Investments in renewable energy, green buildings, and waste reduction could result in universities achieving ambitious carbon-neutrality targets. They might also adopt regenerative practices, contributing to ecological restoration beyond just reducing their own footprint. Campus operations could turn into real-world testing grounds for eco-friendly innovations.

Furthermore, universities could wield their influence to advocate for stronger climate action. Student-led movements and university alliances might transform campuses into epicenters of climate activism.

In this future, universities evolve from mere knowledge dispensers to active participants in climate action. By incorporating climate consciousness into education, research, and operations, they could play a pivotal role in shaping a sustainable world, inspiring not just students but wider communities. This paints a vision of universities becoming key catalysts in combating climate change.

Preparing for Unknown Professions: Academic Adaptations for the Careers of Tomorrow

In the next five years, universities may witness the inception of curricular models emphasizing adaptable skills like creativity and critical thinking, preparing students for unforeseen future professions. Short-term, intensive courses on emergent fields, reminiscent of coding bootcamps, may become prevalent. A decade from now, these models could become a core part of academia, with universities adopting problem-based learning strategies and interdisciplinary studies, creating a balanced blend of technology, social sciences, and humanities. This holistic approach fosters breadth of knowledge and promotes lifelong learning, equipping students for jobs not yet in existence.

Fast-forward fifteen years, and the traditional college major could morph into fluid, competency-based pathways, allowing continual skill and knowledge upgrading. AI might play a key role, predicting emerging fields and advising students on future-proof skillsets. Fields like space-tourism management, augmented-reality experience design, and autonomous systems ethics might be in the limelight, showcasing academic agility. Universities of the future could consistently adapt their offerings in line with predicted employment trends and societal shifts, fostering an academic culture valuing flexibility, continuous learning, and adaptability. They will prepare students for uncertain future careers, launching them into professions we can barely imagine today, but which will undoubtedly shape tomorrow's world.

University of Tomorrow: Navigating a Transformative Landscape

In conclusion, the university of tomorrow stands poised on the precipice of transformation, an institution that will evolve and reinvent itself in response to a shifting demographic, an unpredictable job market, and an unyielding tide of technological progression.

When it comes to harnessing technological advancements, particularly in AI and data analytics, the next few years will witness universities embracing this change wholeheartedly. Automated AI-based advising and data-driven personalized learning will evolve from sporadic implementations to become the standard, much like the path charted by trailblazers like Georgia State University.

In the span of the next fifteen years, the academic landscape is poised for a remarkable evolution. Universities, traditionally seen as bastions of specific disciplines, are on the cusp of a transformative era where the boundaries between distinct fields of study become increasingly intertwined. This evolution is not a mere theoretical forecast but a tangible shift, observable in the rise of fields like bioinformatics. This field, a confluence of biology, computer science, and data analytics, exemplifies the kind of interdisciplinary fusion that is reshaping the academic world.

As we delve deeper into the age of artificial intelligence, a new responsibility falls upon these institutions of higher learning. It becomes imperative for universities to engage deeply with the ethical dimensions of AI. Through rigorous examination of algorithms and a critical eye on data biases, they must incorporate ethical understanding into their curricula. Esteemed universities, such as the University of Oxford, stand at the forefront of this ethical exploration, setting a standard for others to follow.

Looking ahead, the concept of education as a lifelong journey rather than a finite period of study begins to take root in the ethos of future universities. This shift is a departure from the conventional, degree-centric educational model. Instead, a new paradigm emerges, one that champions the continuous acquisition and evolution of skills. This approach, already being pioneered by institutions like Harvard and MIT, prepares individuals to navigate and thrive in a perpetually changing job landscape.

Central to the mission of these future academic institutions is an unwavering commitment to addressing the pressing global challenges of our time, such as climate change and social inequality. By integrating sustainability into their curricula, universities endeavor to instill a sense of stewardship and responsibility in their students, who are destined to become the architects of the solutions for these challenges.

As we forge ahead into this era of rapid technological advancement, the academic world braces for a seismic shift in its disciplinary focus. Fields that once lingered on the periphery, like data science, machine learning, cybersecurity, quantum computing, nanotechnology, and renewable energy, are now advancing to the core of academic offerings. In tandem, there is a growing emphasis on studies that explore the societal and ethical dimensions of these burgeoning technologies, marking an era of thoughtful and responsible technological advancement.

The university of the future is set to be a dynamic entity, constantly reshaping itself in response to technological advancements, interdisciplinary integration, and ethical considerations. This evolution reflects more than superficial changes; it involves a profound transformation in how universities function and contribute to society. They will become key navigators in the complex future, equipping individuals with the skills and knowledge necessary for impactful contributions in a rapidly changing world. Embracing lifelong learning and sustainability, and addressing global challenges, these universities will redefine their role, becoming vital guardians and innovators for the future.

The Final Wager: Academia's Billion-Dollar Gamble

In the rapidly evolving twenty-first-century educational landscape, universities are making strategic choices, akin to a roulette game, where the future is uncertain and the stakes are high. Success in this environment will be determined not by chance but by the ability of these institutions to envision innovative futures, adapt to changes, and take decisive actions. This era of relentless change demands audacity and foresight from universities to navigate and thrive in an ever-shifting academic and technological world.

In a rapidly changing world, the role of universities is evolving. No longer just repositories of knowledge, they are becoming crucibles for developing adaptable and resilient minds. The future belongs to institutions that embrace interdisciplinarity, sustainability, lifelong learning, and ethically guided technological advancement. These universities will lead the way, setting a standard for others to follow, not just surviving but thriving in the face of unpredictable challenges and opportunities.

However, those who resist change, clinging to the safety of the old ways, are poised to lose their stake. They risk producing graduates ill equipped for a digital, automated world, and research that fails to resonate with an environment riddled with complex, interwoven challenges. These universities may face challenges in maintaining their relevance, potentially affecting their reputation, straining their resources, and posing questions about their long-term sustainability.

As we face the tumultuous landscape of economic uncertainty, exploding populations, environmental degradation, and political upheaval, the role of universities as beacons of innovation and change becomes paramount. It's not just about shaping minds and pushing the boundaries of knowledge anymore; it's about arming societies with the tools and insights to navigate the future.

Intriguing Prelude 103

The billion-dollar question remains – will the universities take the gamble and pivot in time? The answer is a matter of survival. As the ball spins in the wheel, the anticipation heightens. Some will stand their ground, betting on their traditional strengths, while others will take the leap, reinventing themselves in the face of adversity.

Like a captivating game of roulette, the thrill lies in the uncertainty. The future of academia hinges on the boldness of its institutions. As the wheel slows, the ball is about to drop. The outcomes will ripple across generations, and the world waits with bated breath. Welcome to academia's billion-dollar roulette. Let the games begin.

References

1 "One of the TAs in an Artificial Intelligence Class Was Actually an A.I.," accessed August 14, 2023, https://slate.com/technology/2016/05/a-teaching-assistant-at-georgia-tech-was-actually-an-artificial-intelligence.html.
2 "Institute for Ethics in AI.," *University of Oxford*, accessed December 30, https://www.oxford-aiethics.ox.ac.uk/.

Index

academia 44, 49–50, 73–80
academic adaptations 100
academic disciplines 86, 98
academic endeavor 99
academic independence 9, 33
academic knowledge 77, 79
academic learning 41, 64
academic opportunities 10
activism 78
adaptive learning 48, 56, 58
Ad Astra 51
adult learning theories 39
Africa 10, 85, 87, 89–91
age of uncertainty 2–3
aging learners 38–39
ally-shoring phenomenon 18
American College Health Association 76
American Council on Education 67
American Economics Review 29
anti-Apartheid movement (1980) 75
AR *see* augmented reality (AR)
Arizona State University (ASU) 67
artificial intelligence (AI) 7, 13, 18, 82, 101; ascendancy, in higher education 52–53; automation and 25; chatbots 51, 96; data privacy and ethical use 51; EdTech 66; educational tools 48, 57; education's hidden pitfalls 57–58; education's promise and perils 56–61; effectiveness of 56; equation 56–57; GradeCraft 66; higher education 48–53; human interaction 57; impact, academia 49–50; integration 7, 49, 53, 66; mentorship 57; personalized learning and 58–59; reimagining teaching 48–49; special education and 59–60; Squirrel AI 56; university administration 50–52
Asia Cloud Computing Association 84

Association to Advance Collegiate Schools of Business 21–22
augmented reality (AR) 65, 83
Australia 12, 41, 88, 90–91; higher education 13; National Innovation and Science Agenda 82; University of New South Wales (UNSW) 63
automation 18, 25, 82

Baccalaureate and Beyond (B&B) 32
bioinformatics 96, 98, 101
birth rates 3, 4, 42; Japan 36; United Kingdom 37
blended-learning models 5
blockchain-encrypted diplomas 66
Bok, D. 6
Boston Consulting Group 19
Brexit 89

Camp fire, in California 41
Canada 12, 40
Canadian Bureau for International Education 12
career establishment 5
career opportunities 5
Carnegie Mellon University 52, 66
Case Western Reserve University 65
chalk-and-talk teaching approach 30
China 11–13, 56, 58, 88, 90; Double First Class initiative 86; e-learning 64; New Generation Artificial Intelligence Development Plan 82; student enrollment, in US 12; Tsinghua University 64; unsettling 12
climate change 25, 41–44
cognitive abilities 76
Columbia University 43
complacency 2
cost conundrum 29, 32–33

cost escalations 29
cost labyrinth 29–30
Coursera 97
COVID-19 pandemic 5, 18, 50, 56, 63, 87, 89; global economy 33; online learning 4, 13, 14; remote learning 23, 57; virtual classrooms 44
critical thinking 3, 6, 23, 77
cross-disciplinary learning 23
Crow, M. 67
cultural competence 75–76
cultural immersion 79
Current Biology 90
curriculum 6, 14, 18, 21, 37, 39; academic 75; homogeneous 58
Cyber-Risk Governance Committee 68
cybersecurity 68
cyber-watchdog 68

data analytics 7
data privacy 51, 59
debt-free public higher education 29
Deloitte Global Millennial Survey 19
demographics 37; aging 43; challenges 4, 86; changes 36, 37, 45; disruption 36–37; internationalization and 85–87; shifts 41–44; transitions 5, 41, 42
"DigitalAccess@Home" Programme 85
digital disparity 84
digital divide 5, 57, 70, 85, 91; Africa 85; artificial intelligence 84; challenge 57; in education 84; privacy infringement 57
digital inequity, abyss of 83–85
digital learning 73, 77, 78, 99
digital literacy 17
digital media 4
digital revolution 63–64
digital storm 67–68
digital Uplift program 63
diversification 13
domino effect 30–32, 36
Double First Class initiative, China 86
DreamBox Learning 48, 58, 59
Duckworth, A. 20
Duolingo 59
dyslexia 59

economic liberalization 11
economic maturity 10
economic mobility 5
Economics of Education Review 28
economic stability 5

economic turmoil 5
economic uncertainties 5
EdTech 49, 66
Education and Information Technologies 60
Education at a Glance 38
EDUCAUSE 51, 53
edX 63, 97
Einstein, A. 15
e-learning 63, 64
endowments 45
entrepreneurship 17
environmental sustainability 41, 66, 79, 98
equity 53
Erasmus+ program 87
Erikson, E. 73
ethics evolution 97
Europe 4, 42, 89; Erasmus+ program 87; mental health crisis 90; universities 10, 12
European Child & Adolescent Psychiatry 90
European Union 58
European University Association 10
experiential learning 23, 40, 96
Experimental Studies in Learning Technology and Child–Computer Interaction 60

face-to-face communication 77
Federal Reserve Bank of New York 29
financial crisis (2008) 5, 6, 10, 29
financial instability 45, 87
financial quagmire 28–29
financial stability 5, 36, 45
financial sustainability 5
fiscal pressures 5
fostering resilience 73–74
Fourth Industrial Revolution 39
Free Speech Movement 74
funding 6, 65; agencies 45; government 78; higher education 29; overseas education 10; private 9, 10; public 5, 9, 10, 78; university 9–11
FutureLearn 64
Future of Jobs Report 17, 23
future-proofed graduates 39–41

Gates Foundation 56
gender-based discrimination 78
General Data Protection Regulation (GDPR) 58

geographic constraints 17
Georgia State University 101
Germany 89; low-carbon economy 41; tuition fees 29
GIGA School Program 82
gig economy 17
global citizens 73
global economics 9–15, 33
globalization 3, 18–19, 25, 85
global trade 9–15
Google: DeepMind AI model 50; Voice Typing 60
government funding 78, 88
GradeCraft tool 66
Gradescope 48
graduation rates 4
great divide 17–25
Great Recession 42
grit 20

hard skills 19, 20
Harvard University 38
higher education 3, 9; artificial intelligence 48–53; Australia 13; China 11; cost of 5, 28, 31–33; crisis 3–7; debt-free public 29; disciplinary structure 23; economic turmoil 5; escalating costs 33; evolution of 69–70; funding 10; futuristic gaze 14–15; India 11; Indonesia 11; leadership 67–68; natural disasters 41; societal progress 75; technology's siege on 65–67; transformation 14; tuition-free 29; United Kingdom 28
Higher Education Policy Institute 4
Higher Education Quality Council of Ontario 24
higher learning 28–34; cost conundrum 32–33; cost labyrinth 29–30; domino effect 30–32; financial quagmire 28–29
HoloLens technology 65
HolonIQ 69
homogeneous curriculum 58
Human Rights Watch 57
Hurun Research Institute 11

identity shaping 73–74
immigration policies 12
income-share agreements (ISAs) 29, 31, 34, 89
India: Byju 56; career options 21; higher education 11; SWAYAM initiative 63–64

Indonesia 4, 11
industry: collaboration with 37; joining forces with 40; partnerships 64–65
inequality 30–32
Infocomm Media Development Authority (IMDA) 83
Institute of International Education 12, 17
intellectual stimulation 38
interdisciplinary learning 3, 96
international higher education 11
internationalization 85–87
International Journal of Child-Computer Interaction 59
International Journal of Educational Technology in Higher Education 49, 67, 77
International Renewable Energy Agency 25
International Review of Research in Open and Distributed Learning 77
international students 6, 10–11, 13, 33, 43; Australia 88; China 12, 14, 86; demographics 33; free education 29; India 12, 14; Japan's Global 30 initiative 86; Saudi Arabia's Vision 2030 strategy 87; South Korea 86
International Telecommunication Union 85
interpersonal skills 76
investments risk 42
invisible loss 75–77
ISAs *see* income-share agreements (ISAs)

Japan 10, 36, 42, 88; demographic challenges 86; GIGA School Program 82; Global 30 initiative 86; Keio University 64
job market 3, 7, 15, 17, 20, 25, 39, 40; artificial intelligence 82; demands 18, 21; supply-demand imbalance 22; unpredictable 101
job seekers 20, 25
Jordan 21
Journal of American College Health 90
Journal of Economic Perspectives 32
Journal of Education Finance 30
Journal of Higher Education Policy and Management 28
Journal of International Students 75
Journal of Population and Social Studies 36

Keio University, in Japan 64
Kennedy, R. F. 31
Kenya 10
K-MOOC 91
Knewton 48, 56, 58
Knowles' Andragogy 39
Kong, L. 67

LaunchLab 65
leadership 6, 43; development 74; higher education 67–68
learning 3, 6; academic 64; adaptive 48; agility 40; cross-disciplinary 23; digital 77; experiential 40; higher 28–34; interdisciplinary 3, 96; online 3, 4, 13, 14, 37, 83–85; personalized 53, 58–59; remote 23; skills-based 40
legislation 78
lifelong learning 6, 7, 37, 43, 91, 97, 102
LinkedIn: pulse check (2020) 20; Workforce Report (2022) 17
loan debt 5, 29, 31
low-carbon economy 41

machine-learning algorithms 48
Malaysia 4, 10, 13
Mandela, N. 30
Massachusetts Institute of Technology (MIT) 13, 63
Massive Open Online Courses (MOOCs) 49
Mastercard Center for Inclusive Growth 17
MATHia 48, 59
McKinsey & Company 11, 40
McVeigh, M. 41
mental health crisis 89–91
micro-credentialing 68, 69
"MicroMasters" programs 40
Microsoft: Dictate 60; HoloLens 65; Seeing AI 60
migration policies 6
Milo 60
Mindler 21
mismatch 17–18
modern academia 2–3
Multi-Institutional Study of Leadership 74
multinational corporations 18

nanotechnology 98
National Association of Colleges and Employers 76
National Bureau of Economic Research 12
National Bureau of Statistics of China 11
National Center for Education Statistics 13, 32, 51, 63
National Centre for Vocational Education Research 83
National Institute for Artificial Intelligence in Education (I-AI) 52
National Postsecondary Student Aid Study (NPSAS) 32
National Science Board 78
National Study of Learning, Voting, and Engagement 73
National Survey of Student Engagement 75
National University of Singapore (NUS) 83
natural disasters 41
neurotechnology 98
new course, charting 63–70
New Generation Artificial Intelligence Development Plan 82
New York Academy of Sciences 57
nonacademic elements fade 75–77
nonverbal communication 77
North Africa 21
Northeastern University, in Boston 24

obsolescence 22
Office for National Statistics 37
OneWisconsin Institute 31
online learning 3, 4, 13, 14, 37, 44, 50, 83–85, 89; effectiveness of 70; flexibility of 78; FutureLearn 64; K-MOOC 91
Online Learning Consortium 53
online paradox 77–78
Open Learning Initiative 66
Organisation for Economic Co-operation and Development (OECD) 38

pandemic's fiscal fallout 87–89
People & Planet 42
personal growth 73–80
Personal Information Protection Law (PIPL) 58
personalized learning 53, 58–59
philanthropy 45
Philippines 4
physical infrastructure 98–99
physical-to-digital metamorphosis 98–99
policymakers 45, 89, 92

political ideologies 6
Pounce 51
predictions 44–45
privacy infringement 57
private funding 9, 10, 33
problem-solving 20, 21, 23
prognosis 44–45
Project Essay Grade (PEG) 49
Psychiatry and Clinical Neurosciences 90
psychological ramifications 76
psychosocial development 73
public advocacy 78
public funding 5, 9, 10, 78; reduction of 29, 33; universities 33
Public Wi-Fi Project, South Korea 85

Qualtrics survey 19
quantum computing 98

Rain Classroom 64
ransomware attacks 68
regression analysis 32
remote learning 13, 23, 57, 98
reputational risks 42
research focus 37
Research, Society and Development 38
RoboKind 60

Sacramento State University 52
Salesforce Authorized Training Provider 24
Saudi Arabia 84, 89–91
Saudi Vision 2030 project 84–85
Science Robotics 60
self-management 17, 40
self-perception 76
shape-shifter technology 65
Sidorkin, A. 52
Silicon Valley 59, 65
Silver Students 38–39
Singapore 10, 37, 84, 87, 89, 91; "DigitalAccess@Home" Programme 85; Ministry of Education 64; SkillsFuture Work-Study Degree Programs 64; TechSkills Accelerator Initiative 83
Singapore Management University (SMU) 67
skill development 97
skills-based learning 40–41
SkillsFuture Work-Study Degree Programs, Singapore 64

skills gap 20, 22, 25, 88
Smart-Campus Initiative 67
smart institutions 50
Smith, S. 14
social development 3, 76
societal change 74
societal digitization 49
societal progression 75
societal shifts 18–19
socioeconomic inequality 31
soft skills 17, 19, 20, 40
South Africa 10, 75
Southeast Asia 4, 10
South Korea 10, 36, 65, 82, 84, 90, 91; international student recruitment game 86; private universities 88; Public Wi-Fi Project 85; Study Korea 2020 Project 86
special education 59–60
Stanford Institute for Human-Centered Artificial Intelligence 66
Stanford University 65
State Higher Education Executive Officers Association 29
stay-at-home degree programs 5
student debt 5, 30–32
Study Korea 2020 Project 86
Study Webs of Active Learning for Young Aspiring Minds (SWAYAM) 63–64
Super Global Universities 92
sustainability 19, 25; environmental 41, 66, 79, 98; institutions 85; practices 99–100

Taiwan 90
technology 3, 18–19, 22; advancements 3, 18, 19, 52, 80, 102; arrival of 98; avalanche 82–83; dominant future 96; evolution of 6; higher education 65–67; HoloLens 65; leveraging 13; mismatch 17; overreliance 59; skills 20
TechSkills Accelerator Initiative 83
tectonic shifts 65–67
Thailand 4, 36
trade wars, impact of 11–12
traditional disciplines 21–22
traditional teaching 7, 14
Tsinghua University, in China 64
tuition fees 9, 33; Germany 29; inflation 29–30; Japan 10
tuition-free higher education 29

110 Index

Tunisia 21
Turnitin 48
UK Council for International Student Affairs 12
unconventional paths 68–69
UNESCO 85
UNICEF 57
United Kingdom (UK) 31, 42, 75, 89; birth rates 37; debt 31; higher education, cost of 28
United Nations 36, 38
United States 4, 5, 21, 28, 63, 87, 90; artificial intelligence 51; automation 18; Brookings Institution report 18; Bureau of Labor Statistics report 30; Chinese students in 11, 13; computing jobs 18; economy 11; legislative and judicial actions 34; loan debt 5, 29; National Center for Education Statistics 38; public universities 30; student loan debt 31; Title IX regulation 78; tuition fees 9
universities 6, 7; artificial intelligence 50–52; Australia 13; budgets 5; challenges 2, 18, 37, 43; China 11; conundrum 22–23; course of adaptation 23–24; crossroads 12–14; crucible of history 74–75; curricula and teaching methods 22; in 3-D 73–80; digital revolution 63–64; economics 9–15; education 99–100; Europe 10; experience digitally 77–78; financial aid systems 34; funding 9–11; future of 79–80, 97–98; global trade 9–15; governments and societies 78–79; industry partnerships 64–65; international students 10; Italy 10; Japan 10; leadership development 74; mental health crisis in 89–91; nonacademic elements of 76; nonacademic facets of 75; online learning 3, 4; operational costs 30; and pandemic's fiscal fallout 87–89; political pressures 6; public funding 33; recruitment playbook 12; reinvention 36–37; repositioning of 70; reputation of 74; research and innovation 45, 99–100; role of 3; self-discovery and exploration 76; Singapore 10; social development 76; societal adaptation 43; sustainability practices 99–100; traditional educational models 23; transformative landscape 101–102; transformative power of 75; vibrant cultural mosaic of 75; Vietnam War era 74

Universities in the Marketplace 6
University of Basel, in Switzerland 66
University of Bologna 4
University of California 41
University of Cincinnati 40
University of Melbourne 13
University of Michigan 66
University of Minnesota 75
University of Mississippi 74
University of New South Wales (UNSW) 63
University of Nicosia, in Cyprus 67
University of Nottingham 13
University of Otago 68
University of Oxford 38
University of Paris 4
University of South Florida 51
University of Sydney 13
University of Waterloo 24

virtual classrooms 44
Virtual Human Interaction Lab 65
virtual reality (VR) 65, 79, 83
vulnerability 18

Watson, J. 49
Western Interstate Commission for Higher Education 42
World Bank 21, 36
World Economic Forum 17, 18, 22, 23, 25, 39, 56, 69

For Product Safety Concerns and Information please contact our EU representative GPSR@taylorandfrancis.com
Taylor & Francis Verlag GmbH, Kaufingerstraße 24, 80331 München, Germany

www.ingramcontent.com/pod-product-compliance
Lightning Source LLC
Chambersburg PA
CBHW051756230426
43670CB00012B/2306